7 PROVEN BEST PRACTICES
from German companies

Thomas Michael Hogg

Book Cover Design: Adriana Longoria

Publisher: tredition GmbH, Halenreie 40-44, 22359 Hamburg, Germany
ISBN
978-3-347-11781-5 (Paperback)
978-3-347-11782-2 (Hardcover)
978-3-347-11783-9 (eBook)

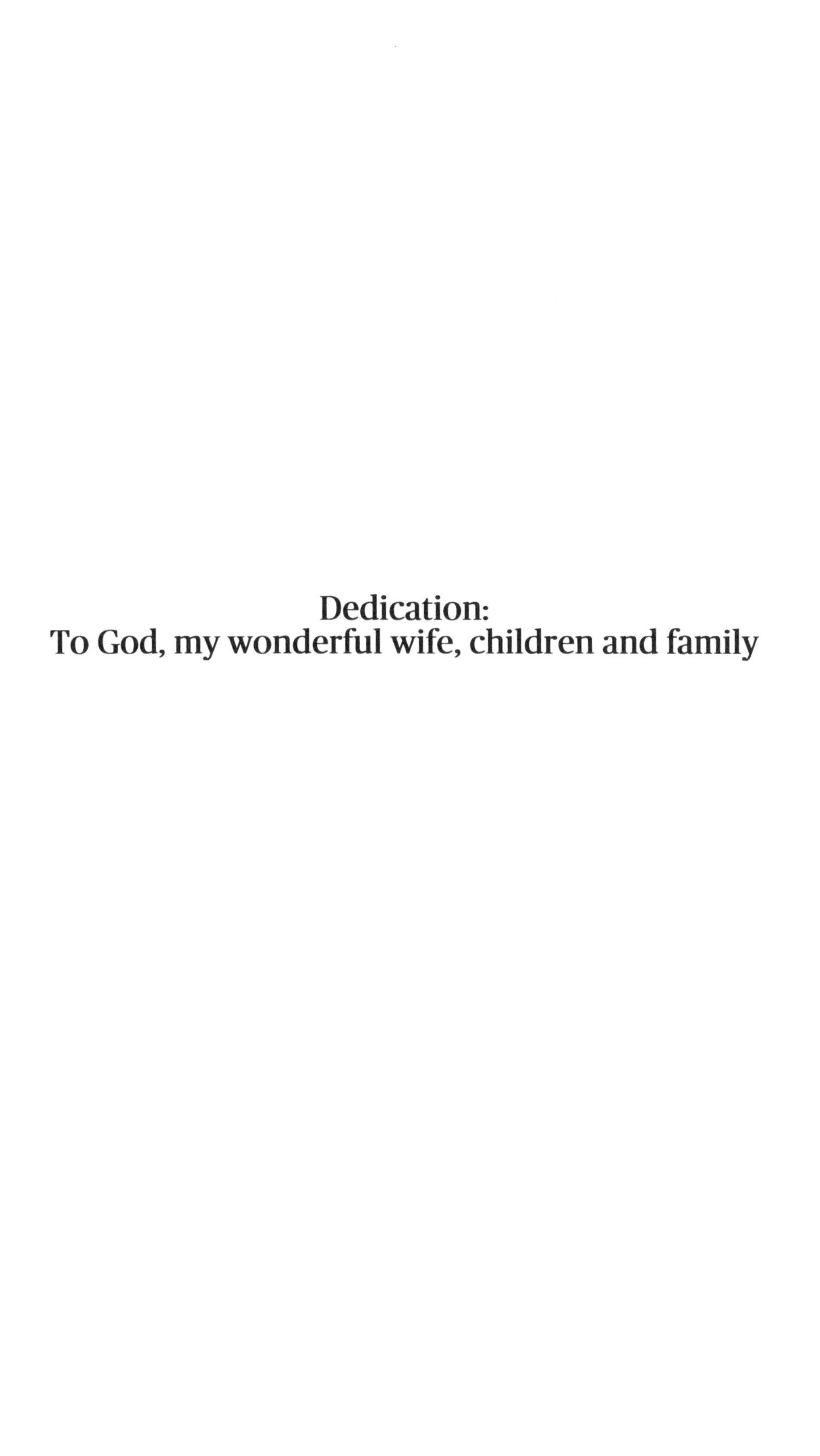

Dedication:
To God, my wonderful wife, children and family

CONTENTS

"Thomas is an excellent strategic planning consultant. His methodology to achieve established objectives is exponential."

Gladiomar Hernandez, Founder & CEO of Hacsys

"Through my experience driving innovation at some of the world's leading innovation companies, I have come to the realization that success of any company or venture is determined by the focus of its strategy and quality of its execution. Thomas Michael Hogg has produced an excellent framework rooted in this principle based on his work with a particular focus on German companies."

Gunjan Bhow, Former Executive at Disney, Amazon, and Microsoft
Global Chief Digital Officer at Walgreens Boots Alliance

"This book is a compass for business leaders in uncertain times. The German industry has distinguished itself for its long-term vision and innovation, concepts that are holistically and brilliantly addressed in this publication. Its goal of guiding companies to a profitable level with healthy finances and growth is successfully described in these pages."

Bernd Rohde, CEO of Hannover Fairs Mexico

"The world's leading economies consist of a wide-ranging source of financially successful companies. The book carries insightful lessons for small and medium-sized companies about the importance of growth and competitiveness."

Lucero Alvarez, Bloomberg TV / El Financiero

"TMH Consulting stands for achieving profitable growth always in an ethical way. This books resumes the way of working of Thomas and his team. Our company improved financially and gained significant market share that made us overcome the crisis."

Rene Elizondo, CEO of Robertson Industries

"This book is very practical and business savvy with human sense. Thomas is supersharp to provide customer and company value both B2B and B2C. A must-read for all SME CEOs and Entrepreneurs who want to learn more about the German specific culture of doing business successfully."

Marcus Koch, Investor, Former Managing Director Redblue

INTRODUCTION

The day to day of a Business owner, CEO or Top Manager gets currently really turbulent and stressful. Delivering constantly to stakeholders or achieving a yearly budget is highly complex, especially in times of crisis. You have to regain and repeat success. You have to outperform over and over again.

In the midst of severe financial pressure and a volatile global economy many companies and managers fail to achieve (high) **annual profitable growth.**

They struggle with both strategy decision-making and strategy execution.

The number of mistakes made and the lack of resources (time and money) allocated to a well-planned and realistic strategy have been one of my essential takeaways on why many enterprises fail.

In 2005, I was one of the happiest persons in the world when I got the opportunity to work for adidas, the global sporting goods giant and world market leader for football (soccer) products. Working day by day with my favourite sport brand one year before the FIFA World Cup 2006 in Germany seemed like a dream come true. I experienced working for and with highly competitive professionals that had the goal to exceed customer needs and quality standards. Furthermore, the company and top management achieved sustainable business results with double-digit growth, especially in emerging countries. At the time, I met Carlos Maza, adidas Mexico Marketing Director, who was boosting sales through a well-defined market penetration strategy and marketing-mix. It was then that I profoundly understood how certain companies grow profitably with a sound strategic plan and execution.

While working as a consultant for PepsiCo, Johnson Controls, Campbell's Soup and several German companies later in my career it was amazing to see how certain decision makers drove and led the growth path of their companies. As always, one learns from the good role models.

In my 20 years of market experiencc I have seen clear patterns, notably of German but also of other international midsized companies, that succeeded on a global scale improving their financial indicators year by year.

This book aims to help CEOs, Directors and Entrepreneurs to focus on certain concepts that will definitely enhance the financial results of your business achieving both solid top- and bottom-line growth.

Therefore, we designed at TMH Consulting a unique **7-step methodology** that surely is going to improve your business results:

© TMH 7-step Profitable Growth Strategy Methodology

Chapter 1 emphasizes on defining and executing on key clients, priorities, people, projects, and tasks bringing you 16x more results. Specific secrets about the quality from German companies is explained in Chapter 2. The target market definition serving a specific segment building a loyal "tribe" is detailed in Chapter 3. Chapter 4 addresses the importance on R&D launching functional products. Chapter 5 gives advice to penetrate international markets with your products and/or services. How to enter the profitable growth zone is covered in detail in Chapter 6. A well-developed plan, a common German habit, will conclude the process to create a more holistic and financially successful business model (Chapter 7).

What are the **benefits** of reading this business masterclass book and putting into practice the 7-step Profitable Growth competencies?

- You will develop critical skills for strategic planning
- You will gain profound understanding of sales and profit drivers
- Receiving clarity for decision making regarding your 2-years growth plan
- Acquisition of new strategy roadmap and execution practices, also to withstand crisis situations
- Gaining insights on how to reach the highest potential of your company or strategic business unit with a sound business mindset
- Reducing stress and uncertainty concerning daily performance pressure
- Improving your ability to achieve financial results

The "TMH Profitable Growth Strategy" book covers elementary tactical and strategic planning, sales & marketing, finance, and management concepts from a completely new and holistic perspective. With this knowledge, you will be able to plan to grow your company above the industry profitability level.

For the past 20 years, my consultant colleagues and I have observed what is working out and what is not. Addressing the Profitable Growth dilemma and delivering business results is our passion, as we know the CEOs are often very lonely and desperate to find the right track to success.

This book is based on what is happening in the real business world and about the challenges company leaders face on a daily basis. A practical approach to bring a company to the next level was the motivator to write this book. This is why, we document the knowledge gained to guide your profitable growth path.

The goal: Entering the profitable growth zone.

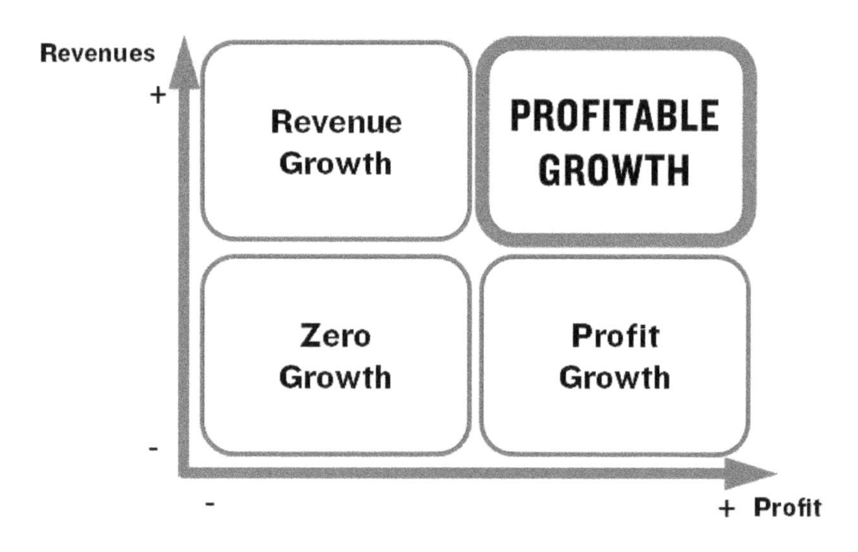

Enjoy reading about profitable growth solutions.

PART I

8020 Focus and No distraction

1 - 8020 Focus and No distraction

Doing a successful and result-oriented job is not as easy as it seems. In 1999, I was stunned by the productivity level and focus of my work colleague at a bank in the South of Germany. Mrs. Müller, a trusted and long-time employee in that bank, was scanning and double checking all high-income transfer receipts. I noticed two aspects at the same time, there were many zeros on each receipt and there were only a few receipts scanned compared to the amount of numerous boxes of thousands of documents. I was confronted the first time with the 8020 concept. All of the high and important transfers were taken into account whereas the majority of transfers weren't included by Mrs. Müller. She only focused on the most important transfers. But as a matter of fact the real lessons learned from her was her focus on time and to deliver her tasks each day in 8 hours because she had a 40 hours week. Every day she performed and there was zero distraction to do what she had to do on her 8 hour-workday. She was delivering concentrated value by simply doing what she was supposed to do.

Sounds like a normal working performance. But, there is one common mistake I see day by day in the numerous offices I visit.

Employees are very often "just not" doing what they are supposed to do.

And even worse, their boss, the CEO, is very often neither doing what he/she is supposed to be doing.

They are trapped in the daily business and the incoming operative problems, mails, social media and non-strategic tasks. They are busier with efficiency than with effectiveness. Doing the right things versus doing things right.

CEO challenge

The key challenge for a CEO is to manage that he/she and importantly his/her team are focusing and executing on the right things each day. And that doing the right things impact financially on profitable growth. CEOs have to define where the company will be in 2 years and not take part in each single decision which his or her managers are responsible for.

CEOs have to define the long-term vision and the fundamental business model elements (for instance closing constant deals with their key account, developing and hiring an outstanding sales team, defining a required service level or establishing a best in class business practice or process) that provide the company a competitive advantage and generate financial value.

CEOs are responsible for the strategy.

Strategy is a synonym for renunciation.
To focus, CEOs have to trade off.

How much time do you spent each day on operational issues?
How much of your time are you in the 8020 zone?

In 1906, Vilfredo Pareto noted that 20% of the population in Italy owned 80% of the property. He proposed that this ratio could be found continuously in the physical world and theorized it might indicate a natural law. For business, we know that in most cases the 8020 rule comes true:

- 80% of work is completed by 20% of your team.
- 20% of your best clients (or customer segment) makes 80% of your sales.
- 20% of your products makes 80% of your sales.
- 20% of your best sales reps makes 80% of your sales.
- 80% of your complaints come from 20% of your customers.
- 80% of value is achieved with the first 20% of effort.
- 80% of project politics come from 20% of your stakeholders.
- 80% of problems originate with 20% of projects.
- 80% of software problems are caused by 20% of bugs.
- 80% of customers only use 20% of software features.

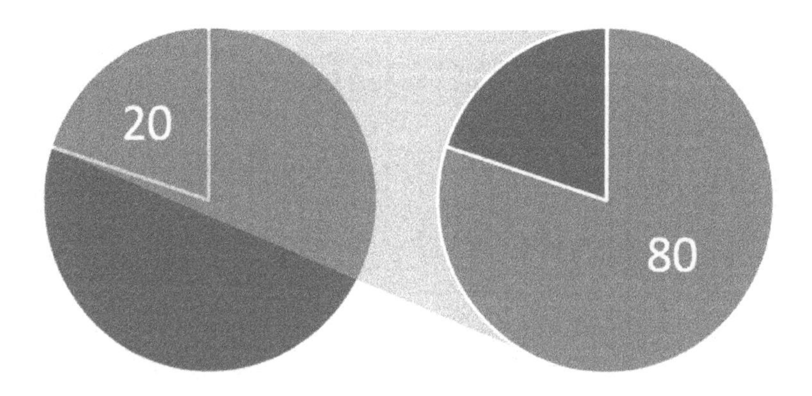

16x Pareto Principle

80÷20=4

20÷80=0.25

4÷0.25=16 → 16x

The right focus with the Pareto principle to define and execute on key projects, clients, priorities, people, tasks, ... brings you **16x more results = impact = success** 🚀

I always include the 8020 principle in all strategy courses I give, as a key part to plan a successful year in order to deliver more customer + employee value and to receive more profitable growth for the company.

Through the years, I have seen that many CEOs, especially of SMEs, lack to see the BIG PICTURE; whereas the most **successful CEOs have become 8020 masters** because they lead their companies to achieve ambitious goals while focusing energetically on the most important actions to reach the higher goals, for instance:

- They visit and develop the relationship of their key clients and prospects to understand market needs and requirements.
- They talk frequently to and retain their key employees, especially key sales people.
- They are aware of disruptive trends and key challenges. Hereby, they are better prepared for an unpredictable crisis.

- They set clear goals and communicate the importance of strategy execution.
- They empower employees and show them the importance of the 8020 rule.

You need to focus perfectly on the 20% that will deliver you the 80% of the desired result. Every decision and action has to be made consciously if our time is used effectively.

These are 8 logic steps to become a successful "**profitable growth company**":

1. Set and remind the sales and EBITDA goals with the majority of your employees and quarterly reward those who achieved them.
2. Focus on high-gross margin projects, products, services and customers.
3. @CEO: Be the number 1 sales guy in the company that inspires customers to buy your products or services.
4. Hire and retain the best sales people in the industry.
5. Develop benchmark and 8020 sales & marketing channels. Very importantly embrace and dominate digital marketing because nowadays every client is digital.
6. Have strong partners and allies that help you to sell.
7. Cross-selling is key. Your adjacencies strategy has to be well defined and executed.
8. Measure and communicate your sales, profit and productivity indicators.

Now, let's have a look at one of the most admired companies in Germany. DAIMLER recently defined the following strategy focus*:

"Four future-oriented fields are set to radically change the nature of mobility: greater vehicle connectivity, advances in automated and autonomous driving, the development of digital mobility and transport services, and electric mobility.

Our objective is clear. We intend to continue to be a leading vehicle manufacturer while developing into a leading provider of mobility services. Every strategic action revolves around one thing, the customer. So also for the future, we will only be as successful as our products and services are in the market.

By means of five closely related components we are pushing forward the biggest changes in our company history - our 5C-strategy. We will be:

- **strengthening our global core business (CORE)**
- **leading in new future fields (CASE)**
- **adapting our corporate culture (CULTURE), and**
- **strengthening our divisional structure (COMPANY).**
- **The benchmark for each of these strategic components is our fifth and most important C: our CUSTOMERS."**

So, defending and strengthening your core business should always be the starting point of your strategy plan, unless you have proven data that your "core business" is threatened to lose more

*Source: Daimler Strategy statement published on the Daimler webpage.
More information: https://www.daimler.com/company/strategy/ (2020)

than 40% of sales and/or market share during the next 2 years. In times of disruption this might be a possible scenario but it is rare especially for medium sized enterprises. The core business is where your company generated the most gross profit during the last 3 years and strengthening this part is essential for maintaining profitable growth for the future.

Your culture and customer strategy focus are two more common key 8020s for every business. Culture is the values that define how everyone acts in your company regarding to customers, suppliers and other stakeholders. One of the most important organizational values is frugality. Rarely found in the today's company values but so crucial for profitable growth. Frugality means the quality of being economical with money. Being prudent and wise when it comes to investment and spending is a must have 8020 value. This is what my dad taught me and how German fathers educate their coming generations. At the end of the day, performance is key and you have to focus without distraction. More importantly, hire focused people.

Business owners are responsible for hiring focused people who are better than him or her and they should not be there to execute 80% of the whole work that by the way only results in 20% of the important results.

Never distract yourself from the 8020 zone.

~~Distraction~~
kills your business.

You and your employees have to be in the 8020 ZONE.

Distraction leads to Procrastination

Please be aware that procrastination means postponing something. It is more and more common in a social world where the new generations loose so much time in consuming social media. But this time spent on video / audio may be out of the 8020 zone. So, a key challenge for Top Management in the next 5 to 10 years will be keeping people focused.

Let's have a deeper look on why people are distracted or procrastinate key responsibilities:

- Too many tasks
- Unclear goals
- Fear of change
- Committing too much
- Fear of failure
- Social media or
- Mainly lack of communication and attention.

Essentially, the communication of the 8020 zone, reasons, goals etc. is going to be more important than at any time in the business history.

Communicate the 8020 principle over and over again, especially internally since it becomes so crucial to focus the millennial and post-millennial employees. Get their attention with creative video and audio messages about the company's 8020 goals and tasks.

Furthermore, a strong focus boosts your company's competitiveness. Concentrate the limited resources where your company excels best in a profitable way. Knowing with which customers, with which products/ services, and in which geographical markets you have already succeeded, gives you a clear hint of where to focus. All the passion and time should be focused on your 8020s.

TMH Case Studies

1

- Failure: Lack of focus. There was a client who had 5000 SKUs and we showed him (analysis-wise) that only 600 products made 80% of sales.

We recommended the CEO to discontinue at least 500 very costly and unprofitable products.

We showed data over and over again. But at the end of day, the Owner did not want to "kill" one single product because these products were like his children and he did not want to "kill" them.

- Lesson learned: Products or services are not your children and you should not have an emotional over-attachment to unprofitable products and services.

Actually, thinking about the biggest failures in the business world, all failures have to do with not taking into account disruptions or that the value proposition became obsolete at some time.

When the big data shows you that certain products do not make sense financially please do consider at least to double check if and why you really should keep this product in your portfolio.

2

- Success: We showed a client data that in terms of geography 80% of his business was in the country's capital since the big companies and budgets were centralized there.

  His headquarters were 600 kilometers away from the capital.

  So, we showed him with data the potential sales his company might have in the next 3 years penetrating the new target market. He decided to move to the capital and among sound B2B marketing strategies we got two new "big" clients, which by the way had the biggest budgets for his products in the whole market.

His 5-years CAGR (Compound Annual Growth Rate) was +200%.

The EBITDA growth was similar.

- Lesson learned: If you have a physical product or you have to sell your service 1 to 1 to real people you have to be close to your 8020 clients and prospects.

  Being in the 8020 zone means your headquarters should be at the target market. 80% of the market value is often driven by only 20% of key players. You and your salesforce have to be close, very close, to your customer.

  This was the success story for this particular client and indeed we have created many of these success stories to be near the target market.

  Oftentimes, the sales representatives are not close enough with their target market clients and prospects. They are physically and emotionally absent.

PART 2

It is all about quality

2 - It is all about quality

"If the industry quality standard is 100, we deliver 150."

This was one of the key lessons learned while working at the adidas headquarters in Herzogenaurach. A remarkable moment for me was seeing the quality testing they did for the products at the adidas laboratory in Herzogenaurach, Germany, the hometown of its founder Adi Dassler.

Quality programme on footballs

- Circumference
- Sphericity
- Shape / size retention
- Water absorption
- Balance
- Weight
- Loss of pressure
- Rebound
- Material

*FIFA Quality programme categories on footballs

*Source: FIFA Quality programme categories on footballs
More information: https://football-technology.fifa.com/en/media-tiles/footballs-testing-manual-2018/

If the FIFA (Fédération Internationale de Football Association) set a quality standard for the soccer balls, many competitors met the standards, but adidas always set the bar of its internal quality standards tremendously higher for quality reasons.

The focus on details when it comes to quality is another German trait. Double-checking every quality detail over and over again is in "our DNA".

Made in Germany

VOLKSWAGEN

MERCEDES

PORSCHE

AUDI

BMW

> *"As a matter of fact, quality is the German trademark. Made in Germany stands for quality."*
>
> **THOMAS MICHAEL HOGG**

Mercedes, BMW, Porsche, Audi, VW when it comes to automakers.
SAP when it comes to technology.
adidas and Puma in the sporting goods industry.
Lufthansa, Siemens, Bosch, T-Mobile, DHL, Nivea, Hugo Boss, Bayer, Allianz and many more are global German quality brands.

They deliver their quality value proposition with outstanding products and services.

At the MISSION STATEMENT ACADEMY website the adidas mission is described with a high focus on boosting the athlete's performance and exceeding expectation.

The reason adidas has a reputation that precedes it is simply because of its uncompromising attitude on quality.

BMW has gradually grown into a global brand due to its focus on quality. Audi is clearly a cut above the rest considering the quality and value attached to its cars.

The SAP quality management vision is to consistently deliver high-quality solutions focused on improving customer satisfaction. SAP is committed to applying the knowledge to enhance products, processes, and services and continually monitoring and improving their performance.

Lufthansa has been certified with the 5-Star Airline rating by SKYTRAX, the international air transport rating organisation. The Certified 5-Star Airline Rating recognises a very high overall quality performance and excellence in ground and inflight product provided by Lufthansa to its customers.

"Quality is a promise to the costumer."

A German product or service often meets and exceeds the expectations of the customers regarding innovations, performance, and quality. Why? There is this engineering and quality DNA we stand for. Furthermore, quality process management is an important task that affects all employees and which can only be executed successfully, if it is fully understood by involved and capable individuals.

Sound quality assurance processes are going to guarantee quality standards and should be developed for three reasons:

- to ensure that the quality standards continue to delight the customer
- to create a benchmark operational standard
- to guarantee that all the everyday jobs concerning quality are fully understood throughout the company and the whole supply chain.

Nowadays, a German product or service still stands for dependability, durability and quality. Furthermore, it stands for punctuality, discipline and success.

Many of my international clients, mainly from Mexico, hold me accountable for these attributes.

At TMH Consulting & Investment Group we have carried out more than 50 customer and industry studies during the last 8 years and when it comes to the 3 key elements for choosing a B2B provider or supplier PRICE has never been the most important. QUALITY and DURABILITY are always among the Top 3 decisive characteristics for customers because quality enables high added-value. High-priced product and service strategies depend on quality as well.

The leading companies seldomly understand value in terms of price. This is essential because they consider a wide range of factors in their price strategy beyond value. As such, it is common for enterprises to associate value and quality. Value = Quality = Functionality of a product or service to a specific customer segment.

But certainly, quality gives you the right to charge more and allows your business to have high gross and net margins. Quality is key for profitability. On one hand, Germans focus on high productivity to reduce costs and on the other hand they focus on quality to generate revenues. And at the end of the day productivity and quality drives profitability. The problem I see is that many businesses do not even measure these KPIs nor they carry out customer satisfaction surveys.

"Customers switch providers due to poor quality."

The truth of top and bottom line results will tell the Business Owners how well the company captured value from making business with customers. The year's end P&L analysis shows you if you had profitable customers. Maybe, it will show you as well that you had crucial 80/20 customer segment. But this is not telling you how bright the company's future will be with current and new clients.

Is your business focusing on delivering quality and relevant value to them?

Do you know the pain points and quality standards of our clients? Do your employees understand the importance of quality and its impact on business results?

It takes many positive customer experiences to negate poor quality left behind from one quality issue.

At TMH Consulting & Investment Group we develop lasting customer satisfaction and quality programs that help companies achieve high customer retention.

6 Tips for delivering a benchmark quality:

1. Design and implement a systematic and periodical quality delivery program.
2. Start with the VOICE OF THE CUSTOMER and ask your key customers in which areas does your company lack to provide the best service and value in your industry.
3. Insist your customer to give you feedback of whether he/she is willing to stay with your brand or company in the next years. Receive qualitative feedback, why your customer is striving to stay with you or willing to leave you.

4. Communicate the results of the survey internally and commit. The feedback should be concluded in an executive summary and a strict quality improvement implementation plan for improvement.
5. Quality on the whole value chain is also so crucial; make sure each element fits perfectly and meets the quality standards. Without very high operations and supplier quality standards long-term success is at risk.
6. Every product / service delivery starts at 0 ("Zero"). This means we cannot trust that everything will work because it did so the last time or the previous years. We are starting at 0 again and aware that we have to take care of the details again and again to maintain the quality level of each new product delivery. The best example here is the AUDI mission*: We act purposefully, systematically and with our full efforts – in other words, consistently. That is why our mission is "Consistently Audi."

TÜV

Quality testing, certifications and delivery are very common for Germans and its roots lies back in the German business history.

The TÜV, which means in German "Technischer Überwachungsverein", is the best example for a systematical approach to quality and control.

*Source: https://www.audi.com/en/company/strategy.html

TÜV Technischer Überwachungsverein*

The TÜV is a Technical Inspection Association that provides inspection and certification services. The origin of this association backs to the 1800, where the industrial revolution came from engineers that had the desire and need that quality and safety standards were fulfilled.

GERMAN INSPECTION STICKER FOR CARS

As of 1950 there is no car in Germany legally accepted on the street without having been inspected by a "TÜV", the official entity assigned by the German government. Every car must be periodically inspected to ensure it meets German safety and quality standards.

*For instance TÜV SÜD https://www.tuvsud.com/en/about-us

The inspection includes a range of the most important functionality features of cars: Braking systems, Frame and bodywork, Exhaust system, Steering and steering wheel, Lighting and light-signaling devices, Wheels, Mirrors and other visual aids, and Seatbelts.

One of the most important TÜV is the TÜV Süd with 1,000 locations worldwide and 24,500 employees providing a holistic portfolio of testing, certification, auditing and advisory services.

MISSION STATEMENT*: "We are passionate about people, the environment and technological progress. We anticipate technological developments and facilitate change – defining standards and going beyond regulatory compliance.

Staying true to our founding principle, we add value by creating a safer and more sustainable future."

VISION: To be the trusted partner of choice for safety, security and sustainability solutions that add tangible value to our clients in a physical and digital world.

TÜV Süd claim "Add value. Inspire trust." represents the essence of the mission statement and vision".

Add value. Inspire trust.

*Source: TÜV SÜD https://www.tuvsud.com/en/about-us/mission-and-vision

So, the focus on quality should be an obsession for your company. A "Quality is King" approach is elementary to have a long-term success. Without quality it is very difficult to enter the profitable growth zone. Loosing quality assures you a sales decline in the future.

~~Content~~ is king.

NO it is not!

Quality is king. Has been and always will be.

Note: In mentioning that content is not king over quality, nevertheless, content is very important nowadays. Content generation is a marketing trend, but there the quality and relevance of content is key. Therefore, quality content is vital and will differentiate your brand in the market.

TMH Case Studies

1

- Failure: The quality and service levels of one of our clients were very volatile. The market benchmark was +95% delivering in form and time.

This metric is often called "fill rate" in operations language and it is used to measure whether a supplier is capable of meeting a specific product or service demand with quality and punctuality.

Due to internal coordination and logistic issues, the company did not deliver the product orders consistently. Sales were going down, especially from one key account.

The volatility of the quality delivery led to rework and 0 "zero" profitability (or even loss) on these projects.

- Lesson learned: Only until the CEO and COO of our TMH client understood the importance of quality delivery of their projects, especially to their key accounts, it was possible to get into the profitable growth zone.

CEOs and COOs have to be aware of the financial impact of service and quality problems. Set standards. The Top Management has to measure the quality and service level the customer gets and the benchmark should be achieving a 98% fill rate. But, it is not only about a %.

Very often it is about perceived quality.

What is the reality of your quality and what is the perception of your quality?

Your client's decision maker has a specific opinion about you and your company. Quality delivery and fostering a trustful relationship are essential for customer retention.

Being a trusted advisor and supplier is not a given. You have to earn and deliver quality in an expected manner.

2

- Success: Over-deliver on a key project with an obsession to improve profoundly the KPIs. Our client's costumer was absolutely surprised on the quality of the product and service:

"We have had many providers so far, but your quality standard was really outstanding."

The Business Owner got many referrals and new top clients in this industry sector.

- Lesson learned: Quality ends up to customer satisfaction and retention, and more importantly to referrals / recommendations.

To be an industry benchmark and reference, your quality is crucial. Your product or service has to meet constantly the customer's expectations.

There are quality management systems out there (for instance: ISO quality standards). Pick a practical one. It is not only about the documentation of quality standards.

More importantly, it is about executing on a high quality level and maintaining that standard.

PART 3

Lead a niche

3 - Lead a niche

Germany stands out for being market leaders not only in the general industries, but also regarding many niches.

The strategy aim is simple: "Be the best in your niche."

Market segmentation is a wise old-school business concept. The secret is to concentrate all efforts on one profitable segment to be the number 1. Positive business results will follow you once you have reached the #1 position.

Leading a niche depends on having a topnotch product or service, but also your marketing and communication strategy is crucial. If you are the number 1 you have to underline this positioning and communicate to your target market: "WE are the market leader because clients and sales say so!"

In my career, I have seen so many companies, organizations and even state governments lacking to market themselves.

New competitors with much lower market share often penetrate the market easily because the market leader "is sleeping" and does not promote its value proposition sufficiently.

I have to admit that in general, many US companies are much better than German companies to market and promote services and products.

But a niche business model does not only depend on marketing.

Useful innovation, operational excellence, and financial management are also highly important C-level topics to lead a niche.

The German "niche" management and business approach has led Germany to become a leader in international trade. Based on economic data, we estimate that German companies are among the Top 4 players in at least 30% of all industries.

The German government and our outstanding chancellor Dr. Angela Merkel have created over the past years a business environment that enables designing and innovating in numerous niches.

Many small enterprises with up to 50 million USD annual revenues are rapidly entering the mid-sized enterprise level with yearly sales up to 200 million USD.

When we talk about German firms leading these niches, we talk about the following sectors: machine equipment, electrical engineering, industrial products, consumer products, automotive & automotive components, construction & building products, pharma and medical technology, high-tech products, chemical products, heavy machinery, software, renewable energies, logistics, among many others.

Würth - A Benchmark company

A remarkable successful company is Würth. I was able to meet the founder's son Reinhold Würth in the early 2000 at my home university at Pforzheim University. It was impressive how he emphasized on the importance of values in his company and family.

Furthermore, the currently 14+ billion Euro company* (regarding sales volume) took many wise decisions from the beginning. The niche, founder Adolf Würth decided to enter, was selling screws, nuts and bolts.

 *Source: Wuerth Finance Investor Relations / Wuerth Group

In 1954, by the age of 19 Reinhold took over. Annual sales = 80 thousand Euros. Market entry: 1962 Netherlands, 1969 the Americas, 1970 South Africa, 1982 Australia, 1987 Asia. The expansion of Würth's international footprint was essential to boost sales.

The strategy is still clearly defined and communicated today on the firm's homepage.

The sales force is the company's heart and soul.*

One of the particular strengths and a key to the Würth Group's success story is the system of direct selling through our sales force organization. Over 33,000 permanently employed sales representatives all over world advise our customers and see to it that craft and industry businesses are offered product solutions tailored to their needs as well as optimal services.

Thanks to **specialization** through the divisions Automotive, Metal, Wood, Construction and Industry, every sales representative is a competent contact in his/her line of business, ensuring individual advice.

This approach makes Würth a reliable partner for its 3.6 million customers worldwide.

*Source: Wuerth https://www.wuerth.com/web/en/wuerthcom/unternehmen/strategie/unserestrat-egie.php

Würth Group's structure provides the possibility to react flexibly to the requirements of local markets and answer to individual needs.

So, specialization (selling to a niche) was the growth secret.

At the end of the day, value is more important than price. Delivering value in a niche segment with high expertise and outstanding service is guarantee for business success.

The lesson learned is being the best in class solution- and service-wise.

~~Selling (too) many products to (too) many customer segments~~ kills your business.

Be the #1 in a niche market.

Be #1 in a niche market.

Becoming number 1 in a niche does not only depend on quality and value, but also on the competence to penetrate a market. This is why sales and marketing are so important. Your marketing strategy and people have to communicate consistently your product and service benefits with the target prospects and customers.

Common commercial mistakes of not penetrating a niche are:

- Marketing budget allocation is low and below industry average.
- Marketing capabilities are not developed.
- The digital positioning is not taken into account.
- Target market is not defined.
- Product/service specifications are communicated, but the customer benefits and value are not communicated.

- The brand has no convincing and sound story (referring to the age of storytelling we live in).
- The sales team does not understand the sales funnel and the goals that need to be achieved at each stage of the sales funnel. The proactivity to knock the right doors and to have a high prospect rhythm is a common root cause of poor revenue management.
- Lack of selling competences of the salesforce. Lack of quality and quantity of salespersons.
- Marketing department does not understand the product.
- One selling and communication approach fits all customers. Maybe, this is another huge Top Management failure. The product and service have to be industry- / sector specific. Each customer segment has different needs and requirements. One size fits all DOES NOT WORK!
- Marketing people talk about branding and sales people talk about revenues. Only common objectives on the sales funnel and steady meetings between the sales and marketing department can build a bridge to achieve a higher profitable growth performance.

A niche player delivers unique solutions and quality content.

A niche player is obsessed with having the best product and service.

A successful niche player serves a profitable market segment.

A niche player is quick what means "high" speed to market. Service is personal and not handled by a robot (referring to today's growth of artificial intelligence robot customer service responses).

A niche player has qualified sales experts.

A #1 niche player is an industry benchmark.

A #1 niche player stands out.

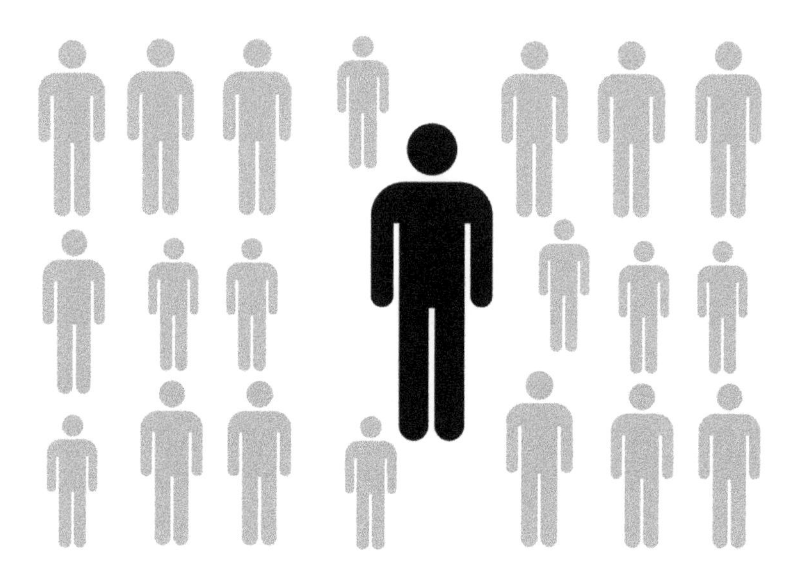

In a recent BBC interview* by Caroline Bayley, Winfried Weber, professor of management at Mannheim University of Applied Sciences talked about “The secret of many successful German companies is that they are hidden champions”.

"In Germany a lot of those small and medium sized companies, also known as the 'Mittelstand', are doing exports from the beginning," professor Weber says.

"They try to be in the forefront of innovation, and find and define a niche, and then sell on an international level."

And the most successful ones are world market leaders in their niche sectors, which Prof Weber says are "hidden champions".

*Source: BBC.com, Germany's 'hidden champions' of the Mittelstand https://www.bbc.com/news/business-40796571

More information on these German "niche" companies:
The success of German businesses is driven by its SMEs, a group to which more than 99% of all firms in Germany belong. Provided that they embrace new trends, particularly digitisation, and that they find ways of recruiting the skilled labour they need, even in times of a skills shortage, SMEs have every opportunity to remain successful in their chosen specialized niche markets. These companies account for more than half of our economic output and almost 60 per cent of jobs. Approx. 82% of apprentices in Germany do their vocational training in an SME.*

As you can see, niche companies often achieve amazing business results and have competitive advantages. Some of the companies might be in a blue ocean for a certain period of time.

TMH Case Studies

1

- Failure: One of our clients had 7 business units and annual revenues of aprox. 3.5 million USD. At this point the Business Owner and CEO at the same time wanted to launch the 8th BU (business unit).

While analyzing sales and profit we found that four business units were struggling.

*Source: bmwi.de, The German Mittelstand as a model for success
https://www.bmwi.de/Redaktion/EN/Dossier/sme-policy.html

Moreover, the working capital was very high and cash flow performance was very poor. The 25 years old company started in a specific niche and the business in this niche was successful.

But, the defocusing on the initial business unit was confusing for the salesforce that had to sell and perform for minimum 3 strategic business unit at the same time. The most profitable business unit, the CORE business, was unconsciously neglected.

- Lesson learned: Often, it is dangerous to neglect the initial business unit and the core business. Neglecting or confusing the customer of your key niche may stagnate the business.

Achieving leadership in a niche is key and maintaining market leadership has to be planned and assured before penetrating other niches and starting new business units. Have you heard a prospect asking: "Ok I listened carefully, but at the end of the day for WHAT ARE YOU REALLY GOOD AT?

The 8020 definition on your business strength is very important. Your brand has to stand for something.

In my case it is very clear that TMH is good at helping a CEO to grow his or her business. This is my personal passion and my highest satisfaction, watching a company and leader grow.

From a small business to a recognized and profitable medium-sized business.

From a medium-sized business to a large corporation that still is customer- and employee-focused.

My passion is designing business models for financial success in an ethical manner.

Or even selling a company at a good price. Our value proposition is clearly defined and understood.

2

- Success: Having a clearly defined target market (niche) was new for the CEO of a technology firm.

The firm had more than 90% of revenue and EBITDA in a very specific industry during the previous 5 years.

The CEO decided to take into account a strategic recommendation to focus on the niche they performed best (sales and profit-wise) and fully committed to defend and strengthen their market share in this niche.

While the overall country's GDP growth this particular year was 1%, the financial results of the company were surprisingly good. 56% sales growth and 32% profit growth!

- Lesson learned: The most common mistake I have seen as a consultant is the lack of target market definition. You have to define the niche you enter and conquer.
  Be the best in class.
  And of course there is a tradeoff.
  You need to be very good in a niche that means in a specific industry, market, geography, demographic, or segment.

  In a larger company where you may have several brands and business units the niche concept also applies. Each business unit / brand should have a specific business plan, market segment and EBITDA goal. Each business unit is accountable to become best in class when it comes to quality and profit.

PART 4

Innovation at its best

4 - Innovation at its best

In November 2014, Dirk Nowitzki became the highest-scoring international NBA player in the history of the sport. Dirk represents certainly quality and this in a certain niche: basketball.

Nowitzki fade away jump

With his innovative **"Nowitzki fade away jump"** he made history and more importantly this innovation won many games and a championship.

"You leave the game in a better place", said Larry Bird after Dirk's last home game after playing 21 years for the same team, the Dallas Mavericks. Dirk Nowitzki leaves a legacy and inspiration for all of us on and off the court. But this remarkable success story and nowadays successful movie* has another main actor: Holger Geschwinder.

Since Dirk was 16 years old Holger Geschwinder was his personal coach and mentor.

Especially, when it comes to innovating new shooting or training methods Geschwinder became a legend.

Physics, rhythmic dribbling with music and other sports like fencing were just some ingredients used to revolutionize the game of his famous student Nowitzki.

His unconventional method concluded in an app "Dirkometrix" where you can calculate and see your own shot from the perspective of the ball to perfectionate your success rate even if the release angle and the deviation to the side are not always 100% accurate.

Thanks to the Geschwinder innovative and practical methods, Dirk Nowitzki became the 6th best scorer of the NBA history with a 31,560 points average per game and the 3rd player with most games played.

The Nowitzki / Geschwinder story is somehow very German because I consider that in general we like analyzing, innovating and improving. This comes true for business.

German "Erfindergeist" led by Chancellor Merkel

The secret behind the most successful German companies is the German "Erfindergeist", the entrepreneur and engineering spirit based on a profound analysis and planning process.

Germany is a Research & Development leader. Right from the top. I was truly surprised being a the opening ceremony of the 2018 Hannover Messe, the most important industrial and technology fair in the world, listening to Chancellor Angela Merkel.

Chancellor Merkel pointed out*: "Germany has to and is going to rise its federal R&D budget to boost innovation, entrepreneurship and the industry 4.0 development. Most importantly, this innovation budget has to be spent on practical solutions and generating ROI."

 *Source: Hannover Messe Opening Ceremony April 22, 2018 (Germany)

Quality comes exactly from this investment in Research and Innovation with a practical focus to deliver quality and value.

> *"New technology is important, but the usefulness and quality delivery of any technology is even more important."*
>
> **THOMAS MICHAEL HOGG**

Some useful German innovations / inventions:

- Aspirin from Bayer
- The ring binder from Friedrich Soennecken
- X-ray from Wilhelm Röntgen
- Contact lenses from Adolf Eugen Fick
- Trolley bus (electric bus) from Werner von Siemens
- The bicycle from Karl Drais
- The car by Karl Benz
- Printing press by Johannes Gutenberg
- Modern refrigerator by Carl von Linde
- Konrad Zuse built the first fully automatic digital computer
- The gas-powered motorcycle by Gottlieb Daimler
- Portable electric chainsaw by Andreas Stihl
- Mercury thermometer by Daniel Fahrenheit
- Rudolf Diesel the diesel engine
- Hydraulic breaker by Krupp
- Theory of Relativity from Albert Einstein

- Nivea by Beiersdorf AG
- Ink eraser by Pelikan
- Glue stick by Henkel
- Fanta soft drink for the German market
- Gummibears by Haribo
- Playmobil by Hans Beck
- Stereobelt, the original concept of the Walkman by Andreas Pavel
- Clarinet by Johann Christoph Denner
- Modern football boots with screw-in studs by Adi Dassler

The importance of innovation for entrepreneurs and CEOs evaluating new ideas should have two aims:

- Practicality
- Customer value

Hannover Messe

Nowadays, German innovations that drive sales and profitability are found in very specific industries. At the most important industrial and technology fair, the Hannover Messe, there is the Hermes Award*, which ranks among the world's most coveted technology prizes.

To enter and to compete for the award, a new innovative solution has to fulfill a very reasonable requirement: **"Products /**

 *Source: Hannover Messe https://www.hannovermesse.de/en/side-events/awards/hermes-award

Solutions are judged to be especially innovative in terms of their technical and economic realization and can make a major contribution to satisfying industrial and/or social needs."

The 2017 HERMES AWARD* winner was German company SCHUNK GmbH & Co. KG. SCHUNK is an international leader in innovative gripping systems. SCHUNK is both an owner-operated German family business and a global player.

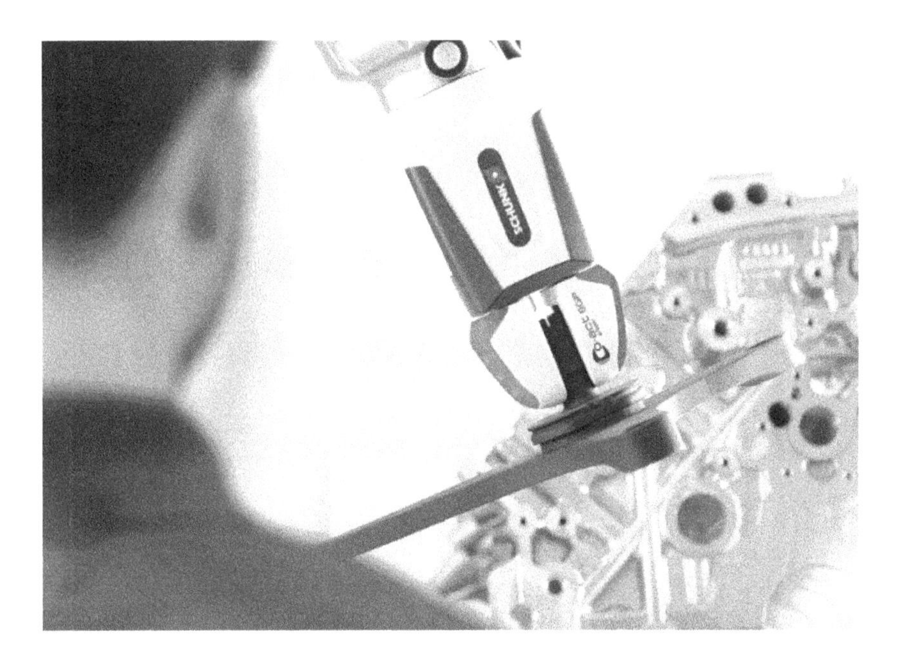

The company's award-winning solution supports human-robot collaboration, making it a vital part of the smart factory tool kit. **SCHUNK**'s JL1 co-act gripper is an intelligent modular gripping system for human-robot collaboration that is capable of directly interacting and communicating with its human operator.

*Source: SCHUNK WINS HERMES AWARD 2017
https://www.industr.com/en/schunk-wins-hermes-award-2283938

The JL1's integrated sensor systems effectively envelop the module in its own safety "bubble" by continually tracking the proximity of humans and triggering evasive action to avoid any direct human-machine contact.

They also enable the module to grip, handle and assemble objects of all geometries. The module's jaws are able to measure gripping force and have tactile sensors, so their operation is highly adaptive and responsive.

The sensor constellation also includes two cameras that enable the gripper to see its surroundings in 3D and help it to detect workpieces. Schunk stands for true German innovation.

Now, let`s have a look at the sporting goods industry and adidas.

At adidas the guiding principle of Adi Dassler, the founder of adidas, is simple: to make athletes better.

That is why, at adidas, innovation is at the core of all our products. The choice of materials and how they are manufactured are the two main ways by which our innovation teams can influence the environmental footprint of our products*.

 *Source: adidas https://www.adidas-group.com/en/sustainability/products/sustainability-innovation/

To mention some examples: Avoiding oil-based plastic helps reduce carbon emissions. Thinner or lighter materials mean less waste and less embedded carbon.

Dry-dyeing clothes saves water, chemicals and energy. Approaching the innovation challenge from an environmental perspective helps us make products that are better for consumers and better for the planet, too.

adidas innovation:

"The ultimate goal is to have a product that delivers high performance, and that is also made in a sustainable way.

Kasper Rørsted, the new CEO from adidas empowered as a strategic direction antother adidas success factor: OPEN SOURCE INNOVATION. At adidas this means to look for all kinds of collaborative creation, not only within the company but also outside the company with athletes, commercial partners, consumers, researchers, amateurs, professionals and creators from many distinct fields.

In the Product Development department at the adidas Football business unit I observed and supported many product tests in the real world with the amateurs. The amateurs tested products and innovations giving valuable feedback to improve the products.

In addition, the adidas *Gameplan A* website and collaboration platform of adidas is a clear sign of open source innovation, not only for product innovation but also for creating a new mindset and lifestyle that in a marketing point of view also is "brand engagement innovation".

➔ Go to https://www.gameplan-a.com/about/

- Join a movement that spreads the values of sport into business
- Get energized and win your work game with an athlete's heart
- Step up and connect with like-minded playmakers.

"INNOVATION without a useful IMPACT is worthless."

TMH Case Studies

1

- Failure: The biggest failure I have seen are CEOs who stick to the exact same business model for decades. 10 - 15 years of doing business the same way is only acceptable when both revenues and profits are growing constantly. But day in day out we see businesses that are in a stagnation phase and most them are small and medium sized enterprises struggling to survive.

- Lesson learned: Without making improvements and innovations you may get obsolete. The velocity of customer demand and upcoming new habits in the digital age are so drastic that many companies won't be able follow.

Strategic innovation sessions and external support on innovation matters are crucial. Having innovation sessions take into account the newest trends:

- The convenience generation
- The super consumer: highly engaged users being more demanding than ever before
- Automated and frictionless buying
- Growth of video and voice tools
- Useful Big data: Future value or Commodity
- Industry 4.0 or even 5.0
- Artificial intelligence, Machine learning and IoT breakthrough
- Salesforce transformation models
- Funnel Hacking
- Recommendation and affiliate marketing
- Digital Marketing
- Earn Trust in an untrustworthy and fake news e-world
- Attention and engagement tools for marketing
- Drop servicing
- Reputation becomes personal branding
- New selling and niche strategies
- Cyber security
- New workplace requirements
- Future of work concept
- New employee education and training models
- Change is the new normal
- Even more political and economic volatility

But at the end of the day analyze and find the 8020 trends that provides real opportunities and threats.

Innovation has to lead the company to future profitable growth; this still remains the main challenge of all innovation efforts.

Keep it short and simple to make better products and products better.

2

- Success: Educating on money and improving the credit rate of employees to maximize their income was the vision to launch a fully digital lending service company. The market was used to time-consuming processes to get a loan. Moreover, some employees were under constant pressure due to financial difficulties.

Employee productivity went down.

At TMH we supported this client to reverse-engineer the complete sales process from the beginning.

We implemented best digital marketing & sales practices on reputation marketing, B2B relationship marketing, relevant content production, copywriting and new sales funnel definitions. Oftentimes you have to innovate on both B2B and B2C selling competencies.

- Lesson learned: Providing real customer value and service pays off at the long-term. The unique value proposition was fulfilled by delighting the employer and the employees with a new service model. But the best product is worth nothing when the sales channel and team are not optimized as well.

Sales innovation is one of the most neglected business opportunities in startups and medium sized companies.

PART 5

Leave the country

5 - Leave the country

> *"If you want to grow, you have to add a 0 to your sales. From 10 million to 100 million. The export revenue strategy is the solution."*
>
> **THOMAS MICHAEL HOGG**

Your business growth strategy only works out when you export your products or at least when you expand your company to new cities.

Another key secret of German companies is their international footprint having a clear plan of how to replicate and scale the business. Each strategy growth plan has to take into account improving your geographical footprint. Growing your company means that you should have a plan that your export revenue share increases above 50% as soon as possible.

There are many entrepreneurs and companies who have a superior product or service, but they stay in their comfort zone and fail to grow. Sometimes it is OK to stay or not to grow if you have other personal goals that have nothing to do with economic growth.

If you aspire economic growth you need to expand.

Open national or international branches, develop international alliances and partnerships, design a distribution model, or selling online on global eCommerce platforms, among other options.

So, specialization, quality and an international footprint design are strategic choices that enable success. The international footprint is crucial to serve customers locally.

Best global quality with local service, always trying to add value and taking care of EBIT margins, is the profound and complex formula to become a profitable growth company. Certainly, a long-term approach is also vital to achieve success abroad. Many companies invest in new geographies with a lack of planning, HR and long-term strategy.

Where and how to grow geographically?

First of all, you need to assure that your product and service may have a probable market acceptance.

Therefore, you study the current competitive landscape and demand.

We oftentimes discover in projects certain markets where there already are potential clients and the competitors do not have an adequate value and service delivery. So, you better take action to conquer that market.

"No one is a prophet in their land."

This is a declaration made by Jesus mentioned in the New Testament in Luke 4:24 (NLT) – "But I tell you the truth, no prophet is accepted in his own hometown." - This is why penetrating new markets probable might be a promising venture.

Many people and markets listen to new proposals when there is value. In business growth is leveraged by augmenting the commercial footprint your company reaches.

Geographical footprint

In order to grow, your company needs to penetrate the market in the biggest city of the country. Moreover, strategic global cities are critical for your growth journey.

Look for key cities and regions to gain market positioning and market share. The best example of a sound 8020 geographical growth strategy is adidas.

"Cities are shaping global trends and consumers' perception, perspectives and buying decisions. We have identified six key cities in which we want to over-proportionally grow share of mind, share of market and share of trend: London, Los Angeles, New York, Paris, Shanghai and Tokyo." *

According to Roland Auschel*, adidas Sales Director, Shanghai serves as a perfect example for the success of the new strategy. Revenue in the Chinese city amounted to 100 million euros in the first half of this year: more than in Austria and Switzerland together.

*Sources: adidas, https://www.adidas-group.com/en/group/strategy-overview/
+ ispo, https://www.ispo.com/new-marketing-strategy-adidas-is-focusing-on-chosen-cities

An international footprint brings complexity but also opportunities.

In our experience, tropicalization is key to adapt and to grow profitable in a new market. Strategic partnerships to get access to a distribution channel and talent will help your company in the beginning. Budget allocation to penetrate a certain market is also important but the company has to set goals and strategies to make your international branch profitable.

Tips for international market penetration

- Finding a trusted advisor or partner from the beginning may save you time and money. Establish a growth roadmap and make scenario planning

- Your distribution and marketing channels have to be planned and executed perfectly

- Take advantage of being "the new kid on the block" to connect to local media, government, associations etc. You will be surprised how many doors open quickly

- Your sales team has to be strong and you definitely need an entrepreneurial leader to start all efforts

- If you already have international customers they are oftentimes delighted to help you enter a new country

- The definition of your target market and a relevant + differentiated value proposition becomes very important. Early pilot projects and trial launches may help you to adjust your strategy

Global footprint of Volkswagen:

In their Volkswagen Strategy 2025+ statement the company underlines its global growth strategy:

"Volkswagen has always made individual and affordable mobility possible for millions of people."

Volkswagen Group and Toyota are the 2 Top players selling more than 10 million cars each year.

In the 2018 fiscal year, the Volkswagen Group increased its deliveries to customers worldwide by 0.9% year-on-year and achieved a new record of 10,834,012 vehicles. The Volkswagen Group recorded sales revenue of €235.8 billion in fiscal year 2018, thus exceeding the prior-year figure by €6.3 billion.

At €17 billion, the Volkswagen Group's operating profit before special items was on a level with the previous year.

With its passenger car brands, the Volkswagen Group is present in all relevant automotive markets around the world.

 *Source: Volkswagen https://www.volkswagenag.com/en/group/strategy.html

The key sales markets currently include Western Europe, China, the USA, Brazil, Russia and Mexico. The Group recorded encouraging growth in many key markets.*

So, what is the most important thing for an effective geographical market expansion?

The most important element for your expansion strategy is your sales team.

Your sales force has to dominate strategic sales competencies like:

- Strategic focus
- Target market definition and penetration
- Knocking doors
- Relationship management
- "Hustle"
- Goal-orientation
- Communicating benefits rather than features
- High price selling focus
- Listen 80%, Talking 20%
- Product and solution knowledge
- Customer acquisition and retention

*Source: HTTPS://ANNUALREPORT2018.VOLKSWAGENAG.COM/

The sales force is responsible for 90 percent of the success of the entire company.

Würth Group achieved 14,272,000,000 Euros global sales in 2019.

"The sales force is responsible for 90 percent of the success of the entire company. The IT specialists are behind it with five percent, and all the rest also five percent," said the 84-year-old company patriarch Reinhold Würth to the German Press Agency in January 2020.

This is why with 84 years he is still on the road with sales representatives. More than 40% of all employees are sales reps.

The Würth Group Sales rep job description:

As a Sales Representative it is your job to drive sales and to grow business with existing customers, selling products and services, while also seeking out new opportunities through identifying, generating and developing new customers.

*Source: WÜRTH GROUP ACCORDING TO THE PRELIMINARY ANNUAL FINANCIAL STATEMENT, https://www.wuerth.com/web/en/wuerthcom/unternehmen/zahlenundfakten/zahlen.php

We equip all our Sales Representatives with the necessary tools to achieve this aim (car, phone, iPad, product samples and literature etc.) alongside continuous support from managers and internal functions.

As a Sales Representative success brings freedom and liberty, there are no limits to your achievement.*

TAKEAWAYS:

1. Geographical expansion needs a long-term vision but a short term action plan.

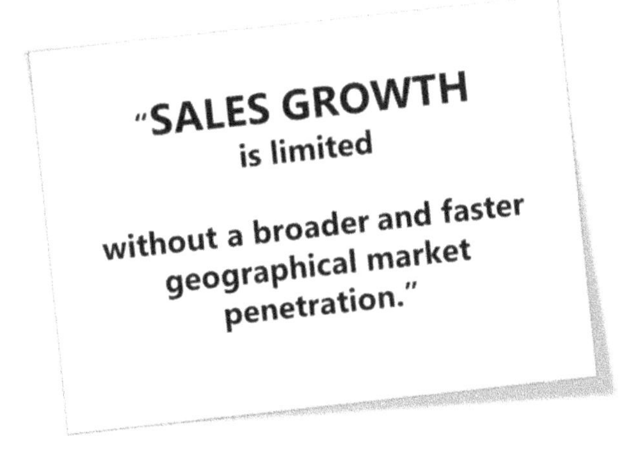

2. Without planning and partnerships market entry is highly complex.

3. Communication of your new relevant market offer is key to build trust.

*Source: WÜRTH Wuerth Career website: job_areas/workinginsales/sales

4. Demand planning and convincing service delivery have to be taken into account for a successful launch.

5. The new complexity brings financial challenges.

6. Your quality has to exceed current competitors standards.

7. Your salesforce needs to be top notch = best in class.

TMH Case Studies

1

- Failure: A company owner moved into a new town. High expertise and product knowledge was a given. The decision was to launch a former high-selling product there and to allocate a high budget for marketing and the grand opening.

  Previous market sizing was on the To-do list and showed a very low sales potential. The real market opportunity was not there from the beginning. Nevertheless, the product was launched and ended being a costly venture with a financial loss involved. The cost of failure and the cost of opportunity were high. Furthermore, the new product manager involved family members on the payroll list without any raison d'être.

- Lesson learned:

Market sizing and investigation are two very important first steps before entering a new market.

A gut feeling or a will to conquer a market often helps to be successful. But when you have strong data that there is no market for your product your investment might be a mistake.

2

- Success: We recently participated as an advisor to open a new branch for a German company from Baden-Württemberg that is a global market leader in a very specific niche in the transport industry supply chain. To meet the global expansion plan their new office in Monterrey, Mexico was key to access the Latin American market.

- Lesson learned: The company had its first Mexico office in another city. Changing the Mexican headquarters near to the key target market gave the company the opportunity to accelerate market penetration.

A second crucial step for success was identifying key decision makers presenting them the innovative and effective solutions never seen before in the local market.

A sound digital marketing strategy was implemented as well to position the brand and to acquire qualified leads.

PART 6

Invest, capture and save money

6 - Invest, capture and save money

Profitable growth is a consequence of delivering quality and serving to customers better than anyone else in a specific niche.

Every strategic three year plan has to include a strategic finance plan where the EBITDA (= Profit / Cash flow) goals are well defined and pursued.

When we talk about money regarding Germans, we always try to create and construct based on what we have. You don't always have to allocate and spend huge budgets in order to progress. Often investment in marketing, innovation, structure and processes is crucial, but we know as well that each year many Managers waste indeed a lot of money on unnecessary ideas, projects and resources.

"Germans are good at not wasting money."

- Thomas Michael Hogg

Trust is good, but control is better

There are so many reasons about why and how companies waste money. This has to do with two things: lack of planning and lack of control. A sound and well planned budget allocation and control are a key profit driver.

A well-known German saying goes:
"Trust is good, but control is better."

Management control is really essential for business success. Not only for the commercial and operations department, but also for financial controlling.

In my earlier working days, I was part of “Sparkasse”, one of the biggest commercial banks in Germany. The daily control of financial indicators was impressive.

At SMEs (Small and Medium sized Enterprises) the financial Key Performance Indicators (KPIs) are often misused or not established.

Spending on marketing and sales is crucial, and you have to measure if this has an economic impact. And of course you do not have to reinvent the wheel, there are already "finance-related" marketing and sales funnel metrics out there.

- Y2Y sales growth
- Gross Margin (%)
- Gross Margin growth ($)
- Market share
- Target market penetration rate
- Customer Lifetime Value
- 8020 marketing channel ROI
- ROAS

So, by transforming your business into a profitable growth company the finance plan and metrics are indispensable.

For many decades the German IT giant SAP has been the most important enabler of German businesses and companies.

The IT innovations on finance and productivity deliver a breakthrough for growing companies. The CEO metrics dashboard design and control is crucial for any organization.

If you lead a for-profit organization "capturing value" is highly important. Having set clear top- and bottom-line goals (topline = sales, bottom line = profit) you can then push your employees to achieve those goals. Create a culture that focuses on profitable growth.

If there is profitable growth for the company, there will be economic growth and better salaries for the employees.

In our TMH top management seminars we underline all these KPIs, but I remember a very remarkable comment of one of the participating CEOs:

"Even if we know our goals to capture value ($), we often don't go after them or we don't share them in a consistent way."

Saving money is a good German habit, too.

Schaffe, schaffe Häusle baue.

"Work, work, .. and build a house." This is a common saying from the Swabian region. Working hard, saving money and then building a house was also my goal because my dad and grandpa did so, as well.

German entrepreneurs often achieve their profit goals because they spend wisely and they save money to build the future.

Historically speaking my parents and I still grew up benefiting from the "Wirtschaftswunder" (German for "economic miracle"), the rapid reconstruction and development of the West Germany economy after World War II.

Without a doubt, the miracle could have not taken place without the generous and strategic economic assistance of the USA to help rebuild West Germany. The Marshall Plan, also named as the European Recovery Program, was a U.S. program supporting Western Europe following the devastation of World War II. Starting form "zero" meant doing more with less.

But of course, without certain funds to invest and to rebuild the country in terms of infrastructure, industry sectors and companies the "Wirtschaftswunder" would not have taken place. Moreover, trade agreements were made to diminish trade barriers and to leverage the economic development plan. West Germany achieved to improve its economic output at tremendous rates. The high capital investment rate thanks to low consumption led to higher living standards and purchasing power.

As real incomes rose, the same way sound government tax income rose, and this fast-tracked the rate of investment and spending in more and more productive projects for both the companies and society. Some projects were: streets, hospitals, libraries, theatres, schools, universities, parks, railway-stations, airports, and museums.

General lessons learned that are deeply inherited in today's German business culture are having a plan with key ingredients like:

- Setting goals
- Investing (spend) wisely
- Spending on / invest in the future
- Do not forget to save for bad times
- Generating growth

In which zone is your company today?
In which zone should your company be tomorrow?

To capture the value of your company's performance you have to deliver profits and cash flow.

Without a sound profitable growth focus of all top employees that are responsible for the business success it is impossible to sustain your organization over a long-term period of time.

Profitable Growth zone

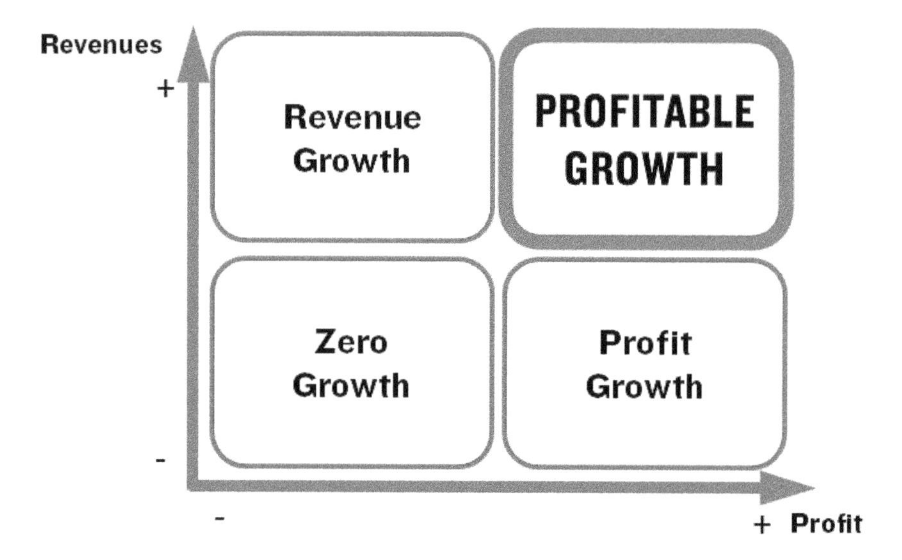

In my experience more than 2/3 of all companies out there struggle to reach or to stay in the PROFITABLE GROWTH ZONE. One key reason is the lack of financial awareness and understanding of the business owner and employees.

But nevertheless, the weakest asset of **un**profitable companies is their sales and marketing department. In a recent study we asked CEOs which area was the weakest one: 54% answered their Sales & Marketing department, while 46% referred to Operations, HR and Finance.

During the last years I learned many profitable growth lessons and a profitable growth company has to:

- Develop the best sales team in the industry
- Hire and develop the best professionals

- Deliver quality
- Achieve best-in-class productivity level
- Be relevant innovatively
- Have a sound geographical footprint
- Compete fiercely (but always with respect and ethically)
- Think long-term
- Save your Compete earnings and invest a part of it again "for new growth"
- Implement a finance and profit culture
- Challenge the political leaders to create sound economic development strategies. Perhaps, this is a tedious task but necessary.

~~Money~~
is there to spend it.

NO it is not!

MONEY is there to invest it wisely for a better future.

A company that has been in the Profitable Growth Zone during the last years is SAP.

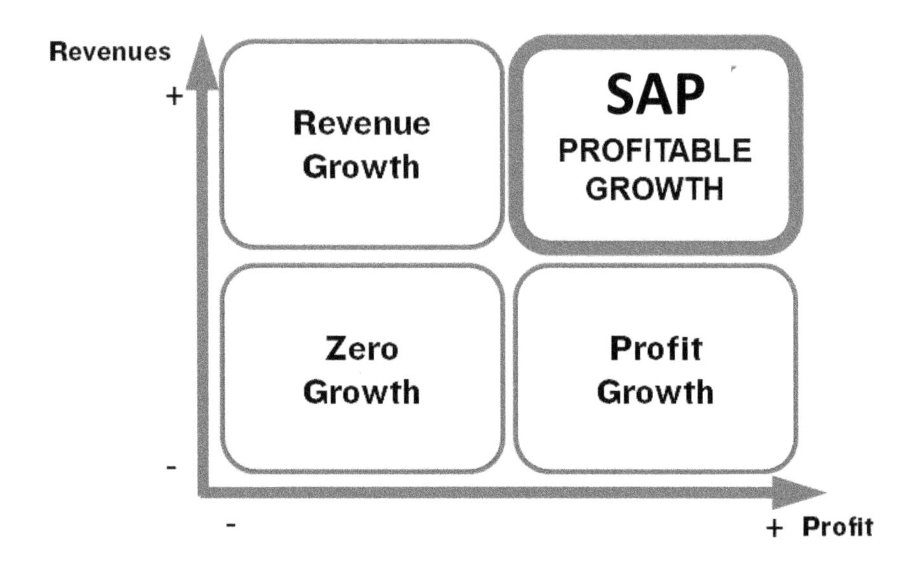

REVENUE

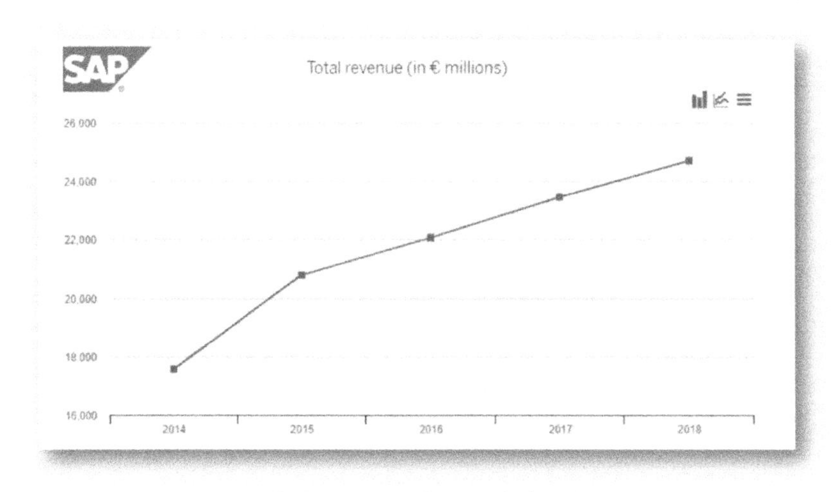

SAP Investor Relations platform*

PROFIT

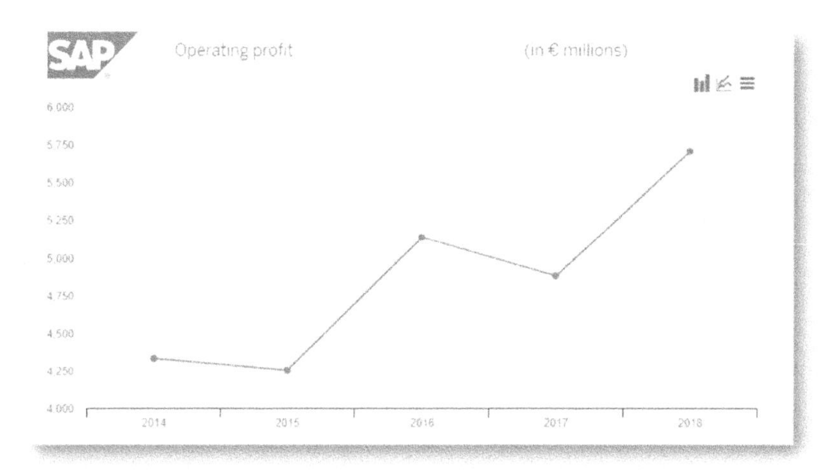

SAP Investor Relations platform*

The German IT giant is a very good example of how the focus of delivering a higher productivity for its clients through SAP products and services results in profitable growth.

Revenues grew from 7.5 billion Euros in 2004 to 24.8 in 2018. They intensely focus on the outcomes for their customers because improving the metrics or KPIs of their customers conclude in an improvement of their own metrics. The best product design, delivery and functionality are essential SAP business model factors. SAP develops solutions and a unique workforce concept that results in customer loyalty, profitability and growth.

So, investing wisely, capturing revenues, and saving money gives companies strong financial strengths, thus creating a virtuous cycle for profitable growth. The financial step of the Profitable Growth practices is certainly essential because without financial success any business methodology is worthless.

*Source: SAP Investor Relations platform https://www.sap.com/integrated-reports/2018/en/interactive-chart-generator.revenue-and-profitability.total-revenue.html

TMH Case Studies

1

- Failure: It seemed that one of our clients had had a really successful year when we looked at the annual accounting report presented by the Finance Director of the company. There was this crucial moment when the CEO asked him during the meeting:

  "The numbers show there is 19% EBITDA. But where is the money? In our bank accounts I do not see the millions of dollars of earnings we generated based on your report."

- Lesson learned: EBITDA is basically net income with interest, taxes, depreciation, and amortization added back. Overall, the accounting reports may show you income and earnings, however that does not mean that the supposed cash flow generated is there.
  Business owners have to firmly document where the earnings are going and where the earnings are:
  - Bank account (savings account)
  - Investments
  - Re-investments

  It may be a dashboard or a simple xls-document. You need a sheet where your earnings are documented with exact $ numbers.

  This is so important to really have a successful handling about investment, savings, profitability, money and $ cash.

  Invest, capture and save money systematically with a plan and periodical report to see:
  - **Where is the money?**
  - **Where is the money going to?**

Ask your finance director: "Where is the money?"

Or even better tell him/her: "Show me the money."

2

- Success: 35% sales growth in 2018, 40% sales growth in 2019.

  2018 EBITDA growth: 50%
  2019 EBITDA growth: 60%

  In one project our consulting team worked with the #**CEO** to focus on profit growth.

  They had a truly successful profit performance and real **profitable growth**.

  The company had a very good value proposition and high customer satisfaction.

  The secret to be financially successful in business means having profitable growth.

Therefore, financial metrics have to be chased:

- EBITDA goal per month in $
- EBITDA goal per quarter in $
- Annual EBITDA goal in $
- Collected revenue goal per month in $
- Collected revenue goal per quarter in $
- Annual revenue goal in $

- Lesson learned: Not only strengthen the value delivery of your product and service, but also design a clear sales and profit performance plan.

PART 7

Plan, plan, plan

7 - Plan, plan, plan

The number of mistakes made and the lack of resources (time and money) given to a well-planned and realistic strategic plan are essential reasons why many enterprises fail.

In fact, it all begins with a strategic plan. But, it is important to first understand the 6 prior steps (described in this book) to design your "Profitable Growth Company Plan".

Focus on long-term sustainability is another German business trait that involves planning and collaboration.

Germans plan where the company should be in 3 years and where should the company start tomorrow. What to offer for whom, how to communicate + market our value, and how to deliver and serve.

A strategic plan

A strategic plan is a systematic process of envisioning a desired future, and translating this vision into broadly defined objectives and a sequence of steps to achieve them.

But why is strategic planning so important?

1. Without strategic planning there is
No plan = No objectives = No focus = No Strategy = No success.

2. Being good at strategic planning will help you see two steps ahead of your competition and keep the upper hand.

3. Strategic planning is the set of managerial decisions and actions that determine the long term performance of an organization.

I have seen so many enterprises fail during the last ten years due to the absence of a well-executed strategy plan.

In the planning phase it is very interesting to see how today's big and successful companies have evolved during their history. Notice that almost every company in the world started way smaller as you may imagine.

We all remember the garage where Bill Gates started the Software giant Microsoft. Stanford University graduates Larry Page and Sergey Brin started Google by leasing a garage for their Google startup, as well. In all these success stories you will discover the brilliant strategic plan / idea after some years of market experience, in some cases more conscious in other cases less conscious planned to change the business world. This means your strategic plan might emerge over time. Strategy planning certainly gives you a competitive edge.

Weinheim, Germany, 1st of April 1972 is the place and date SAP was started by five former IBM employees (Hopp, Wellenreuther, Hector, Tschira and Plattner) with a vision of launching a standard software for businesses. SAP means Systems Applications and Products in Data Processing Services. The plan was to change profoundly the Enterprise Resource Planning and create new value for their clients.

Now 48 years later, with being a Business and Data Management Software leader with so many global customers, SAP has been leveraged by the pioneering essence that inspired its founders to continually transform the IT and business world. Do you want to leverage your business?

First of all ask yourself, what is the vision? What is the one key objective that moves the company to the next level? What are your financial goals? What are your differentiators and what are key elements you have to plan? How should your employees act each day? What are the values and behavioral standards?

Remap your objectives

VISION

- Your vision has to be crystal clear describing the company, company size and geographic footprint in 3 years.

OBJECTIVES

1. Sales objective in 1, 2, and 3 years
2. EBITDA margin
3. Differentiators of the company´s value proposition. How do you play differently successful?

CORE BUSINESS

- Where is the company best at? In which industry with which customers and products/services we have made 80% of our sales the last 3 years?
- How to strengthen the Core Business?
- How to grow the Core geographically?

- Which complementary products and services to add to our portfolio to meet the next sales level?

REMAP YOUR OBJECTIVES

You have to set clear objectives and always increase your competitiveness and profitability. Decision makers have to go even further as defining the basic vision, objectives and core business. At TMH Consulting we re-define the business objectives in a simple 5-step process considering Reach, Empowerment, Metrics, Accountability, and Precision. Understanding and sharing this "REMAP" definition with all employees helps the C-level to execute.

© Copyright TMH Redefinition of business objectives

1. Reach:

Ask yourself what is the purpose, the reason (the "Why") to impact on customers. Impacting customers means to serve them with an outstanding product, service or offer. One of our clients defined among our advice the "REACH" (the goal) to impact and transform the Marketing practices of AAA companies. The Founder and CEO shared this vision with his team and invited his millennial employees and even some of them centennials to impact and transform their industry in Mexico. The firm had a highly successful profitable growth journey from 2014 to 2019 working for customers like PepsiCo, Telcel (the mobile company of Carlos Slim, the world's richest person on 2013 Forbes' annual ranking), Bridgestone, Bayer or 7-Eleven.

Not only do you need to establish a motivational reach. The REACH needs also clear financial goals (Sales and EBITDA). In order to achieve high profitable growth you have to set these reachable goals but at the same time define a high market reach. This is called the "business vision" in terms of IMPACT, EBITDA, PEOPLE and COMPANY SIZE.

About "company sizing" the questions and objectives are:

- When do we meet the 5 / 10 / 50 / or 100 million dollar company goal?
- Which and how many profitable markets geographically we have to reach out? Which cities / countries?
- Which type of customer do we want to reach out with what product / service?
    - In the old marketing days it was called customer segmentation. Nowadays, the customer segments are called warm audiences or "tribes". This is how Seth Godin describes them in his book: *Tribes: We Need You To Lead Us*.
- B2B: How many high-ticket customers do we need to get?
- B2C: How many "subscription" or loyal customer may we impact?

- To how many employees and their families can we provide a good life financially and work-life balanced? 100, 1000 or more than 5000?

2. Empowerment:

First of all, you need to identify talented (future) A players in the market and hire them.

Trust your employees and empower them with a clear set of reach and expectation of goals to be achieved in a certain time. Empower them with new tools and skills by developing the best system to achieve their and your company's goal.

Invest in concrete goal definition, marketing, sales and finance training so that your employees are capable of taking good decisions and use systems to achieve the company's objectives. Empower your employees not only by letting them do everything they come up with, empower your employees by using a successful system and doing everything to achieve the defined reach and goals.

- What is your playbook and system to empower your employees and to achieve the "reach"?

3. Metrics:

You need measurement and reports of the indicators that enable sales and profit. The so called entry metrics and objectives that lead you to the desired exit.

Structure your new objectives for each area in your department:

BUSINESS FINANCE

- SALES
- COLLECTION
- EBITDA

MARKETING, SALES & OPERATIONS

- Customer Lifetime value
- Customer Acquisition cost
- Customer Service and Recommendation Level

The Balanced Scorecard is a very good framework for measuring organizational performance using a more balanced set of performance METRICS. This concept of Dr. Robert Kaplan of Harvard University and Dr. David Norton was originally introduced in a 1992 Harvard Business Review article and still is a valuable source to understand the importance of connected KPIs.

Still, many companies use only financial performance metrics as a measure of success. The "balanced scorecard" complements financial strategic measures with metrics for each company department that are integrally leading to success.

Furthermore, it is important that your employees understand that there has to be metrics, goals and 8020 actions to achieve to open the $ flow.

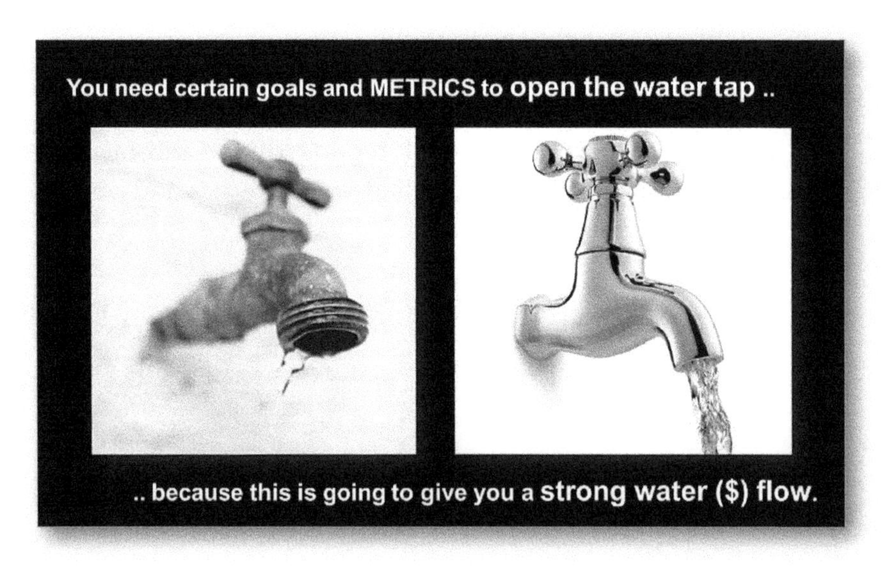

Developing best practices while measuring the right metrics is essential to improve customer value, competitiveness, company growth, and your cashflow results.

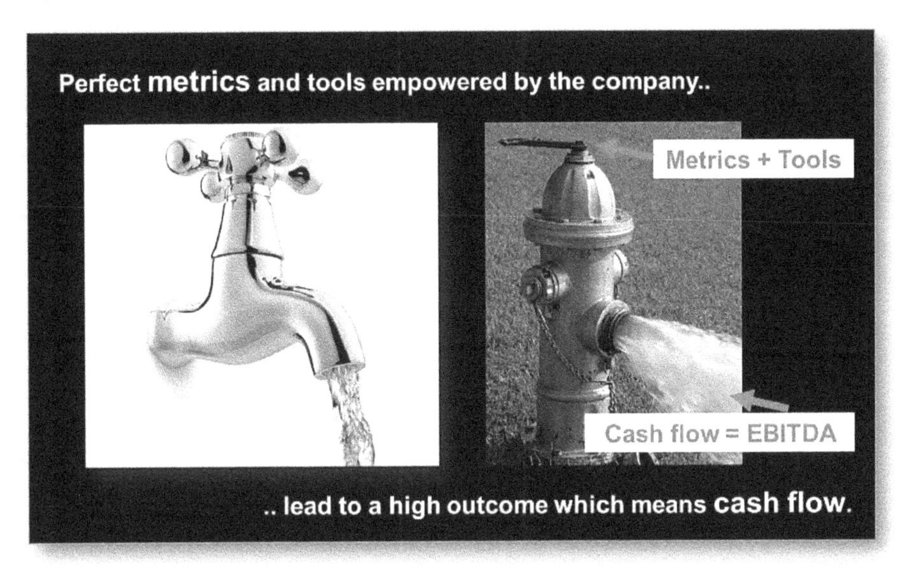

High performance teams are used to working with indicators and see those as part of their toolset. Experts nowadays always need the best tools to leverage and achieve objectives.

4. Accountability: Your employees are responsible of achieving the objectives set from the start which means they are responsible from the beginning of the year or a new project.

Hold them accountable in periodical and punctual meetings. They should create a report describing whether or not they met their goals and why not. And they have to define next steps.

5. Precision: If your set of objectives and metrics are not precise and well-planned, your company will head in the wrong direction.

Precise objectives will leverage the company's growth roadmap.

Precision is also important when it comes to decision taking.

A key strategic decision is to "fire" family member in mid-sized companies and to "hire" professionals who are capable of bringing the business to the next level.

REMAP your business plan and goals at least every 2 years to follow a strategic path, including the profitable growth concept will make your enterprise successful.

Campo Bahia - Plan, plan, plan like the "Mannschaft"

A good example of strategic / tactical planning is the "Mannschaft" (German Male soccer team) of the "DFB" (Deutscher Fussball Bund = German Soccer Federation) from 2004 to 2014.

There was a clear important goal: "Winning the FIFA soccer world cup for the 4th time."

VISION and #1 GOAL:

BECOME WORLD CHAMPION AGAIN

PLAN OF THE "MANNSCHAFT":

HIGH PERFORMANCE WITH A MIX OF EXPERIENCED AND YOUNG PLAYERS

PROJECT AND HEADCOACH CONTINUITY (10 head coaches in 90 years)

BEST PRATICES

CHEF FOR BALANCED NUTRITION

CAMPO BAHIA

Maybe, the "Campo Bahia" was the most remarkable strategy of the 2014 plan. Oliver Bierhoff, the manager of the German team, built a resort with the purpose of giving them extra edge.

Their own resort to relax after the matches and prepare for the next matches reminded us to the German head coach Sepp Herberger who said during the 1954 world cup, that Germany won:

"After the match is before the match."

The legendary coach Herberger was starting to plan the next match immediately when the current match was over. Nowadays, almost every German football has used this phrase and it became a mindset for planning and winning at championships.

Indeed, Campo Bahia gave the German the spirit to win the 2014 FIFA World Cup. Almost everything was planned:

- Construction of houses where 6 players of different teams share one roof
- Community areas in the middle of the resort to connect and improve team building
- Meeting with the local community of fishing village Santo Andre to interact with the Brazilian culture.
- Walk the beach and rest
- Charge batteries for the next match

In conclusion, be aware of the quality of your planning process.

WHAT GERMANS STILL HAVE TO IMPROVE

In an increasingly turbulent world in midst of the COVID-19 crisis, Germany, with its stable structures, its economic strength and a high level of understanding of values, is in greater demand than ever. In the USA there is a "Merkelmania", where many Americans wish to have a prudent and profound leader like her.

Angela Merkel and her government team carried out a never before seen rescue and aid package for the German economy, particularly to support the Small and Medium sized Enterprise segment with tax reduction, cash and direct loan access. Merkel´s leadership to overcome the crisis was remarkable.

As an advocate for Europe and a mediator in international conflicts, Germany should act more and take a leading role. This is pronounced so among 4200 foreign statements about Germany in a recent study of the GIZ (German Corporation for International Cooperation) development agency. And as mentioned in my whole book, Germany has many superlatives.

Some more examples of "Made in Germany"*:

- In Jülich, in North Rhine-Westphalia, stands the largest artificial sun in the world. The spotlights in the laboratory of the German Aerospace Center are 10,000 times brighter than the sunlight on Earth. Here the future of clean energy is being researched.

- In Hamburg-Finkenwerder, the largest passenger aircraft in the world gets its finishing touches: the Airbus A380 is equipped and painted inside in a German plant.

- The world's largest X-ray laser was being built on the outskirts of Hamburg: the European XFEL operates in kilometers of underground tunnel tubes. Researchers from all over the world then explore the secrets of the subatomic world.

*Source: https://bdi.eu/themenfelder/wirtschaft-und-gesellschaft/superlative-made-in-germany/

Maybe, another superlative is the consequence or rather the implications of failing or better said going bankrupt. While in the US, in Silicon Valley investors applaud people who have failed, Germany has the or one of the strictest insolvency laws in the whole world. In the event of bankruptcy, the company boss faces serious civil and even criminal consequences, if he/she does not do everything correctly. This is why, many of my international clients wonder when I tell them:

"You have no choice to fail. You have to do it right at first-hand and you have to be profitable in the first year." This is very German and in fact this is the super-short and super-sharp summary of my whole book.

But hold on a second!

While listing all the goodness of Germany there are so many things we must learn from other countries and cultures.

Some examples of German weaknesses:

1. Digitalisation: In the 2019 Global Competitiveness Index 4.0 of the World Economic Forum we only rank #7.

Germany's biggest weakness is the relatively low level of ICT (Information and communication technology) adoption. Ranked 36th, 30 points away from the frontier, the country ranks behind all the Baltic and Nordic countries, a number of Gulf countries, China and Russia. With fewer than one subscription per 100 people —compared with 32 in Korea and 20 in Lithuania— fiber optic broadband access remains the privilege of the few.

2. Technology: The USA is a world leader in many key technologies, such as military applications, space exploration, biotech, software and computer chips.

3. Germany's healthy life expectancy of 69.5 years is one of the shortest among European nations and five years below Singapore's.

4. Ecology: Germany is no longer a #1 ecological model. The Environmental Performance Index (EPI) is a method of quantifying and numerically marking the environmental performance of a state's policies. Switzerland #1, Germany #13. I think it is important to become a more "greener" country. Air quality #46. Climate & Energy #64.

5. Declining working population from 2020 onwards, despite immigration.

6. Venture capital landscape versus the USA limits productivity gains. Venture capital deals in the United States and China tend to get the most attention. Startup fundraising deals are much more common in the USA and the UK.

7. Among the Top 3 business schools (MBAs) in the world you may not find German universities.

Some crucial homework has to be done and it is important to question the status quo and never think your way of doing things is superior.

Well, again as Germans we have to be so careful not to get trapped by our historic errors or by arrogance, but at the same time we have to understand our core "how to make business" practices and improve them continuously, being open for international advice and collaboration.

COVID-19 SCENARIO

COVID-19 scenario

The Profitable Growth Strategy book launch was postponed several weeks due to the COVID-19 pandemic. A never seen before crisis that showed which companies (and countries) were better prepared and acted rapidly. For me, it was clear that I wanted to include the advice I gave to decision makers during these tough times.

94% of the companies "cross-industry" were negatively impacted due to the global COVID-19 crisis.

This was the result of a C-Level study we carried out at TMH Consulting during June 2020. In certain countries, Mexico is the case, government support for Small and Medium sized Enterprises was insufficient and was provided too late. So, the challenges for the companies were tremendous, especially in terms of liquidity. Cash flow problems became even worse due to rise of late or no client payment. 62% of the CEOs mentioned that the expired portfolio (account receivables) went up.

I was mentioning many when not all of the seven principles (chapters) we addressed in this book during customer meetings. The strategic "crisis" recommendations for Business Owners and Top Management of course have to do with the 8020, financial planning and strategy.

So, what should have been the C-level response?

1. → Push for (target) market share growth. The most #**important** Top Management task is to maintain and grow the market share in their industry. During a crisis it is easy to gain or lose market share depending on the agility and financial stability of each market player.

2. → Defend your #**CoreBusiness** and key clients sales. Serving your key customers means "key"!

3. → Transform your business model, especially your financial model focusing on cash flow and profitability.

4. → Improve your #**competitive** position through improving substantially your service level.

5. → Organic and market-relevant #**innovation** impacting the business model.

6. → Inorganic #**growth** if financial and cashflow situation allows so.

7. → #**Divest**. Or close certain business units. Especially companies without financial reserves and without access to debt.

The productivity and competitiveness challenge is tremendous. The new situation is a financial disruption and will change the rules of the game.

WHAT IS YOUR TOTALLY RELEVANT #postcrisis VALUE PROPOSITION?

Service and value **delivery** becomes more important. Your operation strategy has to set new service standards for differentiation.

#**Customer** and lead generation strategies have to be innovated by providing relevant content and a clear ROI for new investments in any project.

#**HR**: Employees have to be much more effective. HR training has to show and provide a short-term benefit for the business.

#**DecisionMaking** has to be more holistic financially-wise and service-wise. Management has to assure 8020 focus and results.

The #**CEO** has to be more involved than ever to push all areas and employees to a new productivity level.

As any crisis there will be winners 👍 and losers 😒

Four Lessons Learned:

1 **Do not lose market share**

Every sector has its specific dynamics and crisis implications. Without any doubt some industries were severely affected.

Survival of the fittest means having strong $ reserves and effective + agile decision taking.

Consolidation of certain markets will be a logic consequence. What's your plan for a post-crisis market share growth?

2 **Engagement+**

Assertive communication with a sound handling and sensitivity of the difficult situation may boost engagement. Brands with a holistic employee, client and society value delivering will win new "brand lovers". What are you doing to connect with your "tribe"? Any "wow" value included?

It was amazing to see the response of Deutsche Messe AG. They had to cancel one of their most important global fairs in April, the before mentioned Hannover Messe. But they launched in July a new concept called “Hannover Messe Digital Days” with more than 10,000 registered participants. This 2-day digital event certainly engaged with key customers and visitors.

3 **Cash flow and scenario planning**

Companies, even SMEs, with a more profound finance control and planning processes have a clear competitive advantage during a crisis.

4 **After the crisis is before the crisis**

It is not the first nor it will be the last crisis your company will face.

Many enterprises have to close forever, so the winners who survive and transcend certainly had some key competitive advantages: Better agility, better Finance KPIs, better practices, better Fill Rate, better people focused on 8020, better access to loan / credits, among other variables.

What are your lessons learned?

In complex and difficult times we need the right attitude to make our lives and others more successful.

We have to take responsibility to adapt a positive attitude.

We need an attitude that inspires others around us. Yes, it is so difficult but it will be even more difficult with a bad attitude. A positive attitude changes almost everything and opens the door for a better tomorrow.

Let's believe that better times are ahead and with the lessons learned in this difficult and challenging times we will come back stronger.

Don't lose hope for a better tomorrow. Hope is a belief in a better tomorrow. Start every day with a new hope because there's always hope for a better tomorrow. Choose hope. Choose performance. Choose to shine.

EXECUTIVE SUMMARY

Executive summary

It is all about developing a new growth mindset around the 7 competencies we thoroughly studied in this book.

Business owners and CEOs have to establish a set of these attitudes, habits and competencies because these seven concepts are the enablers of profitable growth.

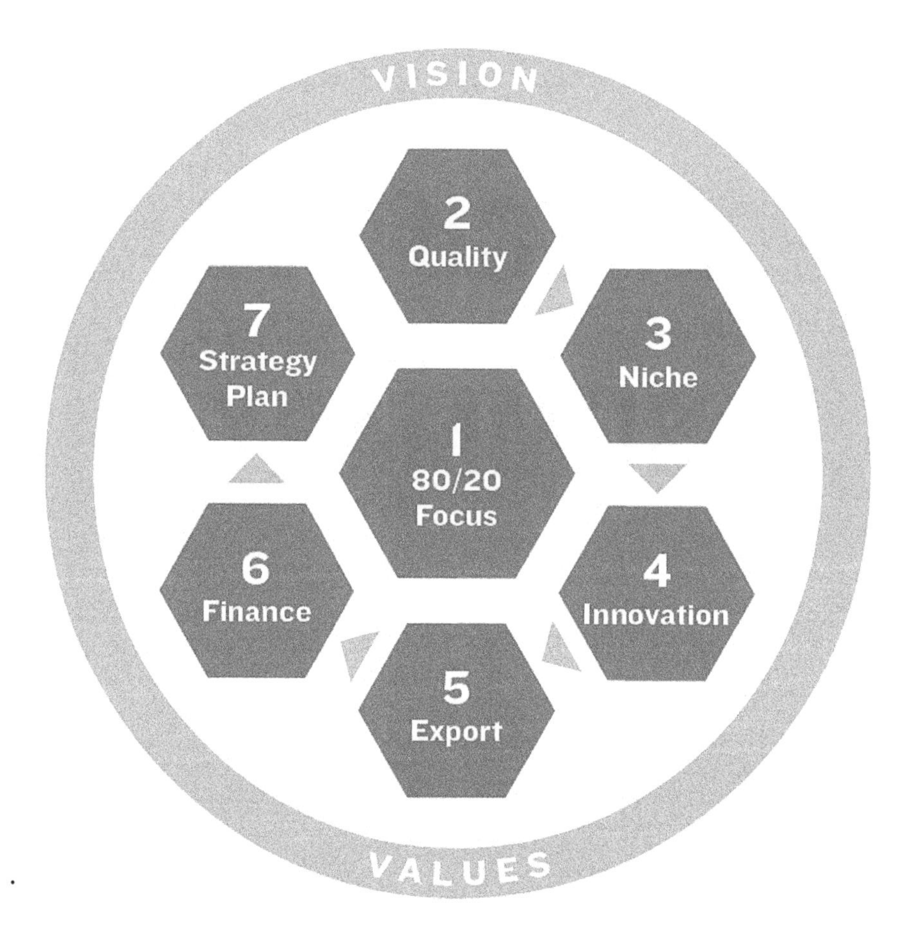

© TMH 7-step Profitable Growth Strategy Methodology

Before executing successfully your profitable growth strategy, the company's vision and values need to be (re)defined carefully. The vision statement and the financial vision determine the scale of your business. Set a clear direction and strategic objectives.

Furthermore, the company's values are a game changer when it comes to constant performance and ethical conduct. Well-developed and well-communicated employee principles concerning behavior and actions set your enterprise apart from the competition. Additionally, strong principles inspire to achieve being an outstanding employer brand.

Profitable growth is not just a business term, it should be a mindset.

There are many books, courses and business school classes on innovation, quality, finance and strategy however there are very few or none on profitable growth.

Growth is part of almost every enterprise at a given moment. But, achieving a constant profitable growth is the number 1 challenge for Business Owners and CEOs.

Maintaining market leadership with a high market share (+15%) in a specific market niche is possible!

Focus, quality, segmentation, innovation, internationalization, profitability and planning are 7 lessons to enter the profitable growth zone.

7 proven best practices from German companies are:

1. Focus on what is relevant for your customer, employee and profitable growth.
2. Give importance to quality.
3. Serve a niche, a specific customer segment, tribe, community better than anyone else.
4. Modernize your business with relevant innovations in several areas, for instance product development, customer journey, service delivery etc.
5. Boost growth with an export strategy of your product / service.
6. Understand the profit drivers and have a finance plan with several scenarios: optimistic, conservative, and crisis-mode.
7. Verbalize and execute the strategy with a clear plan.

Surely, you have already made a certain progress in some of these 7 steps. But the challenge is to analyze, plan and execute holistically on each task of this 7-step framework. And at the end of day, people make the difference. Therefore, be sure to have a qualified and motivated workforce and well-defined structure to execute.

In my experience, the next step should be an as-is analysis and a to-be profitable growth plan. It may be an individual analysis or a workshop with your executive team.

Therefore, you will find in the next chapter a method to implement your own analysis and synthesis on profitable growth.

PROFITABLE GROWTH AUTO-ANALYSIS & PLAN

Profitable Growth Scorecard	Our company does not meet expectations "Poor performance"	Our company partially meets expectations "Below standard"	Our company meets expectations "Industry level"	Our company exceeds expectations "Benchmark level"
1 8020 Focus				
2 Quality				
3 Niche				
4 Innovation				
5 Export				
6 Finance				
7 Strategy				
Total Score				

Scale:

- 1 = "Poor performance": Our company does not meet expectations
- 2 = "Below standard": Our company partially meets expectations
- 3 = "Industry level": Our company meets expectations
- 4 = "Benchmark level": Our company exceeds expectations

Discuss the seven topics with your executive team and board members.

Each one of the participants needs to assess the seven Profitable Growth competencies form a scale to 4 (strongest) to 1 (weakest) to analyze where the company stands today (AS IS).

"AS IS"
CURRENT SITUATION OF COMPANY X

Profitable Growth Scorecard	Our company does not meet expectations "Poor performance"	Our company partially meets expectations "Below standard"	Our company meets expectations "Industry level"	Our company exceeds expectation "Benchmark level"
1 8020 Focus	●			
2 Quality			●	
3 Niche			●	
4 Innovation			●	
5 Export			●	
6 Finance	●			
7 Strategy		●		
Total Score	**2.3 / 4**			

Weakest competences on this mentioned case "company x":

- 8020 Focus ("There are many distractions that affects our Core business", "Lack of focus of Sales Director and insufficient Marketing budget to penetrate our target market")
- Finance ("Our finance / EBITDA goals are only communicated and incentivized to the top management. We had severe cash flow problem during the crisis. Decisions and actions made by our middle management does not impact sufficiently our desired results")

Strongest competencies:

- Quality ("Customers appreciate our quality standard")
- Export ("Our geographical footprint is broad")

"TO BE" PLAN
FUTURE: WHERE WE SHOULD BE

Profitable Growth Scorecard	Our company does not meet expectations "Poor performance"	Our company partially meets expectations "Below standard"	Our company meets expectation "Industry level"	Our company exceeds expectation "Benchmark level"
1 8020 Focus			●	
2 Quality				●
3 Niche			●	
4 Innovation			●	
5 Export				●
6 Finance			●	
7 Strategy			●	
Total Score	3.2 / 4			

Leverage your Profitable Growth strengths and improve your weaknesses with a sound action plan (defining What, Why, How, When and Who).

7 POSTS FOR PROFITABLE GROWTH

8020 Focus

~~Distraction~~
kills your business.

You and your employees have to be in the 8020 ZONE.

Quality

~~Content~~ is king.

NO it is not!

Quality is king. Has been and always will be.

Niche

~~Selling (too) many products to (too) many customer segments~~ kills your business.

Be the **#1** in a niche market.

Innovation

"INNOVATION without a useful **IMPACT** is worthless."

Export

"SALES GROWTH
is limited

without a broader and faster
geographical market
penetration."

Finance

~~Money~~
is there to spend it.

NO it is not!

MONEY is there to invest it
wisely for a better future.

Strategy Plan

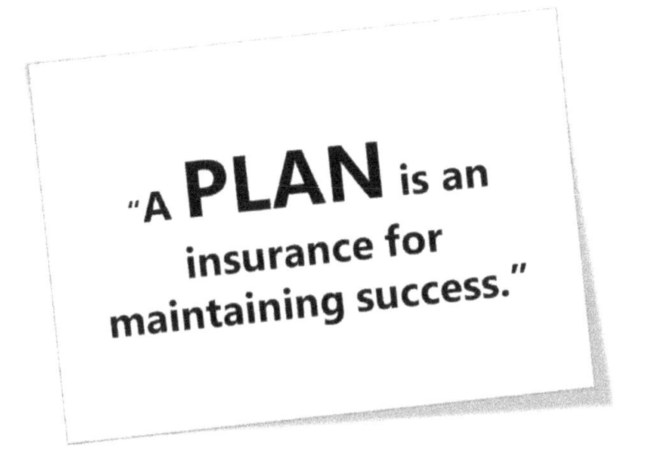

Why profitable growth is important?

Profitable Growth gives the company a VISION of lasting and re-investing. Profitable Growth is made for shareholder and employee value. Pushing the business and transcending as a brand at the same time is possible, even being an employer brand.

Is profitable growth (financial focus) contradictory to an employee focus?

We live in a HR world and the importance of people-focused enterprises to not only generate company value but also employee value. In other words, being an employer brand while meeting all shareholder goals. Is this possible? Yes it is and with common profitable growth goals meeting the financial objectives there should be a sound budget allocation for all HR strategies. But the question should be rather if employee value creation can be fulfilled without profitable growth. The answer is a clear "No". A company without profitable growth is not able to invest in people.

MY LESSONS LEARNED AT adidas

My lessons learned at adidas

In 2005, I worked in Herzogenaurach, a little village where Puma and adidas come from and still have their global headquarters. From my experience at adidas I know that sports and business have a lot of things in common and might impact your future results. Working for and with top executives of the German sporting goods giant adidas, I learned 4 crucial "P's" that profoundly influence my business thoughts and decisions until today.

There are four highly important elements to be successful in business and that key decision makers at adidas take into account:

- PASSION
- PERFORMANCE
- PROFIT
- PURPOSE

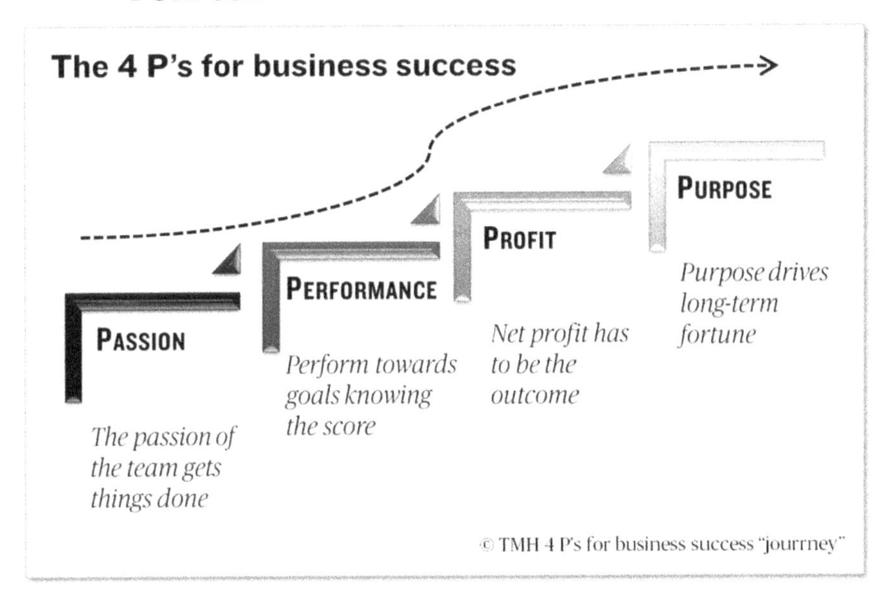

In your everyday business challenges you probably have asked yourself about these four elements. If not, it is time to think about: How passionate are you about what you do?

Do you perform according to results and expectations? Are you and your actions, decisions, and strategies profitable? Does what you do or decide have to do with the real purpose?

PASSION

Sport is about passion, and there is no successful athlete that is not passionate about what he or she is doing. Athletes breathe, live, and dream what they are doing every day. Most of them make their dream come true doing what they love. Are you passionate about your job, responsibilities, projects, objectives, and team? Your teammates will notice it and your results will show it as well.

At adidas, passion is a way of working and thinking. So was adidas' Founder Adi Dassler, he was not only passionate about helping the athletes perform, he wanted them to perform BEST. The best example was his innovative idea at the 1954 Football World Cup in Switzerland, which allowed the "Miracle of Bern". Germany was still affected and devastated due to World War II, a time, we as Germans are very ashamed of. In 1954, Germany still had to cope with many issues and certainly it seemed that we neither had the pressure nor the team to win the World Cup. In the first round Germany played against the football giants and best player of the world Ferenc Puskas, scoring a goal, at the 8-3 victory over Germany. But, both teams advanced to the final.

Germany was losing 2-0 in the first half, and only a miracle or rain could change the result. But both of them happened in the second 45 minutes.

And this is where Adi, who was in charge of the equipment of the German National team, came in. He provided the players with an innovation never seen before, a whole new boot made out of thinner, lighter leather and with screw-in studs.

While the Hungarians struggled during the rainy final wearing heavy rain-soaked boots with studs that were too short to find a grip on the muddy field, the German team went on to score the game-deciding goal with more grip and a better feel for the ball.

The famous scream "Rahn schiesst.. TOR TOR TOR!" from sports reporter Herbert Zimmermann became legendary, it meant that Rahn, the German goalgetter of the team at the time, scored the decisive 3-2.

Germany won its first "Soccer" World Cup. Interestingly, the German team traveled home to Germany by train. And the first stop the train from Switzerland made was Singen am Hohentwiel, Germany, my native city.

My grandpa told me how they welcomed the champions at the train station giving them gifts. The passion for the sport was born thanks to the passion, innovation and entrepreneurship of Adi Dassler.

This is why, the victory brought new confidence to our country, for adidas and Adi Dassler, the innovative football boots brought international recognition and a market leadership in the football business.

PERFORMANCE

Performance is certainly another crucial ingredient to be successful. Therefore, we have to consider both, individual and team performance. Without individual performance there is no team performance. Do you perform best? Do you have the skills to leverage your business becoming number 1?

Ask yourself as well: Do I really help my team? Where can my team perform better? Do we use best practices or do we set best practices? Top athletes and teams always improve and perform towards a desired result.

At adidas the performance factor plays a crucial role on and off the field. Here are some examples. At 07.00 am, before starting work they meet to run together, at lunch time they play soccer or tennis, and at the end of their workday they use the headquarters' gym. Thereby, the sport performance is automatically inherited in the firm's culture.

Moreover, employees are performance-driven because they know that they have to develop the best products to satisfy the demanding athlete's needs. One example at the adidas headquarters is Aubrey Dolan, the man responsible for creating the lightest boot in football history. Dolan describes that they identified a clear need for a speed boot and designed a holistic concept to make the players faster on the pitch.

Another self-reflection: Do you perform best to satisfy customer needs? Do you perform to win?

Perform to win, this is what Herbert Hainer, the former adidas group's CEO, mentioned on the 2015 company's strategy updates: "One factor of strength that stands out is our towering desire to win. Believe me: you can witness it in pretty much any meeting as well as in any match on one of our headquarters' courts and pitches. It's in our DNA."

PROFIT

Even though, many athletes and business people are working hard, many of them lack to be profitable. Profitable means being productive and of course WINNING. At the bottom line, are you really winning each week, month, quarter or year? Do your business decisions and projects really generate profits?

At the adidas' headquarters there has been one really good decision talking about the Mexican Market. In 2006, the Mexican

Football Federation (FMF) was looking for a new and reliable partner, while adidas was looking for the market leadership in the Mexican sporting goods sector. At the world cup in Germany the adidas' decision makers were surprised by the amount and passion by the Mexican supporters.

In Nuremberg, close to the adidas headquarters thousands of Mexican fans made a huge impression during the FIFA World Cup match and 3-1 victory against Iran. Therefore, the key Sports Marketing executives of adidas in Herzogenaurach took a long-term win-win decision. They signed a long-term agreement and a profitable business with the FMF that had its peak at the 2010 and 2014 FIFA World Cup where the Mexican jersey was one the most sold SKUs. adidas is always looking for real and long-term partnerships that deliver profits for all parts: athletes, the federation, and for the firm. Not surprisingly adidas is focused on maintaining its position as the world's leading soccer brand.

This is why, the company recently announced that it has extended its contractual relationship to support the Mexican National Team through 2022, what seems to be an ongoing profitable project for all parts.

Even though profits are the bottom-line and crucial for the German firm, former adidas' CEO Herbert Hainer considers another decisive success factor: the purpose of the firm. "We have a clear purpose: sport. Everything we do at the adidas Group is rooted in sports. Sport is our very purpose," Herbert Hainer.

PURPOSE

The firm's purpose is not only serving athletes, federations, and customers, but also taking care of your own talents, your employees.

It was very surprising that adidas did not fire key employees during the economic crisis 2008 and 2009, while certain competitors did so. adidas trusted its talents, knowing that it is like sports: Even if there is a downturn you may come back even stronger sticking to your mission, people, and core values.

The whole company is focused on the adidas group mission statement to be innovation and design leaders, consumer focused, dedicated and most importantly a global organization that is socially and environmentally responsible, ..

*Source: adidas 2012 booklet.
https://www.adidas-group.com/media/filer_public/2013/07/31/adidas_gb_2012_en_booklet_en.pdf

and is financially rewarding for our employees and shareholders.

Passion and Performance are the key ingredients to deliver outstanding Profit and stick to your Purpose.

Let us know what you think about the 4P's and your experience about these four important pillars at your company.

ABOUT THE AUTHOR

About the Author

Thomas Michael Hogg is Consultant and Mentor with more than 20 years of market and work experience in Germany, Mexico, Switzerland and the USA.

Thomas is a columnist at El Financiero. He has been featured in Bloomberg TV, CNN Expansión, Milenio, Reforma, Negocios en Imagen, Mexico Industry, Cluster Industrial among others.

Thomas has been an advisor to global companies as PepsiCo, adidas, Campbell's Soup, Johnson Controls, Bulkmatic, among other multinational companies, SMEs and nonprofit organizations. He also has been consultant to the State Government of Nuevo Leon Mexico and the University Tec de Monterrey.

Thomas is Founder and Managing Director of TMH Consulting & Investment Group (www.tmh.com.mx) and his business expertise is on:

- Strategic planning
- Strategy and Business Model Design
- Profitable Growth Company Design & Implementation
- Marketing & Sales Strategies (B2B + B2C)
- International Market Research
  (Countries: Brazil, Germany, Mexico, and USA)

Key industry insight:

- Consumer Product Goods
- Sporting Goods
- Retail

- Automotive
- Construction
- Government Economic Politics
- Management Consulting
- Digital Marketing & Commerce
- Furniture
- Education
- Entertainment
- Power & Electronic Industry
- Restaurants
- Telecommunication
- Internet sector, and Non- profit organizations

Thomas has served costumers in projects and coaching sessions for instance at PepsiCo Latin America, adidas group - Germany, adidas Mexico, Campbell's Soup Mexico, Gamesa, Johnson Controls, Secretary of Economic Development Government of Nuevo Leon (Business Nuevo Leon), Bulkmatic Mexico, TecMilenio University, Yancor E-Commerce, yuhu.mx, Industronic, Grupo Aislacon, SiPCo, Rud, Headways Media, Robertson Industries, among others 300 companies.

Thomas is an engaging and thought-provoking keynote speaker for several topics:

- Profitable Growth strategies
- Strategic Sales and Finance Planning
- Strategic Planning for SMEs
- Business Model Design
- 8 strategic selling competencies
- Voice of the customer
- Lessons learned at adidas
- How to increase your competitiveness
- The Marketing & Sales Bridge
- Competitiveness for Mexico
- Designing a successful future in Mexico

A husband and father, former semi-professional tennis and soccer player, Thomas holds an Executive MBA from the IPADE Business School and a Diploma from the Executive Leadership Program at Berkeley from Haas School of Business (USA). He is *Diplom-Betriebswirt,* international graduate of Business Management & Marketing from Pforzheim University (Germany), Tec de Monterrey (Mexico), and Cracow University of Economics (Poland).

Among his social responsibility Thomas has served pro bono for more than 10 years as Board Member at TEDI (Down Syndrome Organization), for more than 6 years at Unidos Somos Iguales ABP and for more than 3 years at Protege tu Corazon.

Furthermore, Thomas gained experience of organizing top management events in Germany, Mexico, Colombia, Costa Rica, Guatemala, and El Salvador. For instance, events carried out with:

- Mexico's Former President, Dr. Ernesto Zedillo
- ExpoManagement, Michael Porter
- Governor of Mexican Central Bank, Dr. Guillermo Ortiz
- President of CCE, Carlos Salazar
- State Government of Nuevo Leon, Fernando Turner, Former Minister of Economic Affairs
- Invest in Niedersachsen Germany, Bettina Boller
- Joachim Elsaesser, Executive at BDI (Industrial leaders of Germany - Association)
- Bernd Rhode, CEO of Hannover Fairs and in charge of Industrial Transformation Mexico
- President of TIC (IT) Cluster of Monterrey
- President of Novartis Mexico, Sergio Duplan
- CEOs of Carrier Mexico, adidas Mexico, Xerox Mexico, Dell Mexico, etc.
- Oracle and SAP
- Facebook
- Amazon
- Google

Sources / References:

1. SAP Blogs, A time for founders, May 13, 2014, https://blogs.sap.com/2014/05/13/a-time-for-founders/
2. Daimler company strategy, 2019, https://www.daimler.com/company/strategy/
3. FIFA footballs testing, 2018, https://football-technology.fifa.com/en/media-tiles/footballs-testing-manual-2018/
4. Mission & Vision| TÜV SÜD, 2019, https://www.tuvsud.com/en/about-us/mission-and-vision
5. adidas Mission Statement, 2013 / 07, https://www.adidas-group.com/media/filer_public/2013/07/31/adidas_gb_2012_en_booklet_en.pdf
6. Mission Statements:
   - https://mission-statement.com/adidas/
     Mission Statement Academy, Information 2019
   - https://mission-statement.com/bmw/
     Mission Statement Academy, Information 2019
   - https://mission-statement.com/audi/
     Mission Statement Academy, Information 2019
7. Strategy audi.com, 2019, https://www.audi.com/en/company/strategy.html
8. Hannover Messe Opening Ceremony April 22, 2018 (Germany)
9. hermes award - Hannover Messe, Hannover Messe homepage, 2019
10. Co-act - gripper HRC SCHUNK, 2019, https://schunk.com/es_es/co-act/pinza-co-act-jl1/
11. SAP Quality Vision, Mission, and Policy, www.sap.com, 2016/01,https://www.sap.com/documents/2016/01/3631f19e-597c-0010-82c7-eda71af511fa.html

12. Lufthansa is Certified as a 5-Star Airline – Skytrax, 2017/12, https://skytraxratings.com/lufthansa-is-certified-as-a-5-star-airline
13. GERMAN FEDERAL MINISTRY FOR ECONOMIC AFFAIRS AND ENERGY, 2020, https://www.bmwi.de/Redaktion/EN/Dossier/sme-policy.html
14. Germany's 'hidden champions' of the Mittelstand - BBC News, www.bbc.com, 2017/08, http://www.bbc.com/news/business-40796571
15. Schunk wins Hermes award, 2017, https://schunk.com/mx_en/news/highlights/market-technology/article/3070-schunk-wins-the-hermes-award-2017/
16. Marketing Effectively To The 'Super Consumer' – Nielsen, 2015, https://www.nielsen.com/in/en/insights/article/2015/marketing-effectively-to-the-super-consumer/
17. 10 Hot Consumer Trends 2019 insights and reports, 2019, https://www.ericsson.com/en/reports-and-papers/consumerlab/reports/10-hot-consumer-trends-2019
18. The Balanced Scorecard—Measures that Drive Performance by Robert S. Kaplan and David P. Norton, 1992/01, https://hbr.org/1992/01/the-balanced-scorecard-measures-that-drive-performance-2
19. Tribes: We Need You to Lead Us (English Edition), Seth Godin, 2019, https://www.amazon.com/-/es/Seth-Godin-ebook/dp/B001FA0LAI
20. The 4 Disciplines of Execution: Achieving Your Wildly Important Goals: McChesney, Covey, 2019, https://www.amazon.com/Disciplines-Execution-Achieving-Wildly-Important/dp/1491517751

21. World Cup 2014: Germany's purpose-built training camp has given them extra edge, 2014/07, Telegraph.co.uk, https://www.telegraph.co.uk/sport/football/teams/germany/10962216/World-Cup-2014-Germanys-purpose-built-training-camp-has-given-them-extra-edge.html
22. Wuerth career homepage, 2019, https://your-career.wuerth.com/web/en/karriere_2/job_areas/workinginsales/sales.php
23. Wuerth finance homepage, 2019, https://www.wuerth-finance.net/web/media/pictures/investor_relations/geschaeftsberichte_wfg_wfi/2018_1/WFG_GB2018_EN_Web_Berichtsteil.pdf
24. Germany Study: Germany in the eyes of the world, https://www.giz.de/de/weltweit/63559.html
25. Superlatives-Made-in-Germany, https://bdi.eu/themenfelder/wirtschaft-und-gesellschaft/superlative-made-in-germany/
26. German Car Brands: www.bna2013.com
27. World's most powerful x-ray laser to be unveiled near Hamburg on Friday: https://www.thelocal.de/20170831/worlds-most-powerful-x-ray-to-be-unveiled-in-hamburg-on-friday

About ProfitableGrowthStrategy.com

ProfitableGrowthStrategy.com published by TMH Consulting & Consulting Group and Thomas Michael Hogg is the premier online source for insight, advice, and tools for growing your company profitably.

The offerings include:

- Online courses based on the book and experience
- Webinars, seminars, conferences, and events
- Memberships
- Studies and research on Profitable Growth strategy and practices
- Newsletter with articles on core topics in strategy and sales

About TMH Consulting & Consulting Group

TMH Consulting is an international consulting firm that designs and implements impact-driven strategies & business models for companies and non-profit organizations. The key services are Strategic Planning, Marketing & Sales Strategy, and Market Research. More information: www.tmh.com.mx

The reader of this book will receive valuable insights, such as:

- How to make profitable your unprofitable business
- How to organize and structure your complex company
- How to help a CEO stop being the bottleneck of the business
- How to make your employees very productive and making your business improve sales
- How to grow your business

In brief, giving structure, focus and profitable growth to a company.

"I really have to say that this highly practical book sums up the basic principles for a successful company with a powerful methodology, concise details and interesting anecdotes. Descriptive, readable and inspiring. I will apply these insights immediately to my new business."

Niclas Seidel, Founder & CEO of Yancor

Lightning Source UK Ltd.
Milton Keynes UK
UKHW040634240521
384271UK00001B/244